AF481096

The Revisionist Volume 2 –

The Torture of Love

By: Michael A. Delitala

Dedication

Dedicated to my wife.
Because after all, all of this had to occur to arrive
to my authentic self for my one and only person.

Table of Contents

Chapter 1

This will be a story about love. Rather, the ebbs and flow of love. Actually, the torture of it. You are human, Dear Reader, and these stories will hopefully make your hearts swoon with possibility. And then an instant later you'll cry with tears of sadness. Maybe you'll cry tears of joy as well. This volume, as The Revisionist, I revisit the past. Past loves that is.

I was raised rigorously which you can read about in Volume 1. That's not gratuitous advertising but it sets the stage for why this Volume is necessary. As a child and after leaving grandma's (my mom) house to be with my dad and his wife, I was not allowed to explore my individuality. I was not permitted to have my own thoughts. If I did have thoughts, I certainly was not allowed to convey them. My brother Ricardo once told me, that, "Dude, you never had a childhood. It was taken from you. You've always been an adult. You were forced to be an adult by those heinous primary and secondary maternal figureheads". So profound and true. And it made me into who I eventually became.

I was raised to believe in God. I don't believe in God. It doesn't mean I don't believe in something bigger than myself. When I was about thirty years old, a book fell into my lap in a bookstore. The title of that book is "Synchronicity". Are you fucking kidding me? Obviously, it was a synchronous moment, and a clear sign that the Universe was reaching out to me. If you're wondering, it fell into my lap because a beautiful brunette woman who was holding the book had tripped, and subsequently, the book flew from her hands where it landed right in my lap. We'll talk about her later.

After I was able to come to terms with and understood what was trapped inside of me, this anger, rage, and sadness, and after reading "Synchronicity", I realized that I needed help. I asked for some help by deciding to make an agreement with the Universe, which is, after all, a synchronous concept.

Here's what I said out loud, which is a critical point to make when you're speaking to the Universe. Three things (I digress, my apologies, Dear Reader): 1) Either speak what you need out loud, 2) write it down or 3) both. Then be patient. But also, you must put the work in. There are no free lunches.

Universe, thank you for this amazing sign. Not that I needed it, but I now know it exists. I have for all of my life felt like an odd individual with not having the same belief system as what seemed like literally everyone else around me. Also, why are they trying so hard to convince me that my belief system has me going to the fiery pits of hell? How can they believe that since there are so many different philosophies with different deities around the entirety of the globe. With their belief, it means everyone on the planet except them are going to that fiery pit. How could that possibly make any sense? Anyway, the only thing I really want from you is balance. Can we agree that with the good, also comes the bad. Can we agree that I know there will be bad and that there is some profound reason the bad is occurring so that I can grow and become more? I'm ready for the journey of life. I love life and live life to the fullest, and I know that means there will be consequences. I know, though, because of our agreement to have balance, that we'll be able to work ourselves back to the good, and it will be even better than before. I need your help. I'm lonely. Right now, all I'm asking for is love. To love someone. To have them love me back.

In high-school, I started to develop a sense of myself. I was a good-looking kid. 75% Italian, chiseled features, had really nice hair, straight A-s, ran track, played football, wrestled, played tennis, basketball, baseball, soccer, and for the most part I was a super nice guy and, I think fairly popular. That said, I matured, physiologically speaking, and hit my peak height of five foot three by the time I reached freshman year. Even back then, I had a great degree of Self-Assurance but I was emotionally retarded, and it was a huge blind spot. I have all this passion but I just could not figure out how to channel it towards the opposite sex. Afterall, I was going to the fiery pits of hell "if I were to ever take it out of my pants". What that ended up looking like was that a lot of my friends were girls but they never became my girlfriends.

I was invited to parties. At parties, I was known for bringing two things, a six-pack of Zima, and a sleeping bag. For those who might not know, Zima was a clear, lightly carbonated alcoholic beverage made by Coors Brewing Company at a whopping 5.4% alcohol by volume. Zima doesn't exist any longer unless Coors brings it back. Anyway, after one Zima, I was cracking jokes and speaking to every beautiful woman at the party. After a second Zima, I'm now offering back and shoulder rubs to every beautiful woman at the party (including those with boyfriends). After a third Zima, I'm fucking horny as hell and trying to get those beautiful girls to make out with me. The 4th Zima, I'm blacking out. And by the fifth I trudge myself to wherever the final destination is, which is of course my sleeping bag. That last Zima, I don't know. I suppose it was up for auction to whomever noticed it was there lying solely by itself and not amongst other Zima friends.

Earlier in the week in the hallway of our high-school, and only a few days leading into a party, I walked up to the most beautiful woman of our class. She was (still is) drop-dead gorgeous. Actually, she became a famous California model for a spell. She modeled during high school, and all of us dudes would go find the K-mart advertisements so that we could ogle her in her bras and panties. I engaged her in a conversation about how tall of a guy would be her type. She's 6'4", I'm 5'3". She says, "I only date tall guys; Sorry, Michael and if you were taller, I'd date you because you're so cute". I say, "Well, that's really unfortunate because actually height doesn't matter. It doesn't matter because after all, we're all the same height when our crotches are aligned". Deservingly, she slapped me across the face but then looked at me with her ocean eyes, stared into mine, and had a flirty grin after she had stopped laughing hysterically. I had piqued her interest.

Then, there's the party. I followed my usual Zima recipe, and after Zima number 2, I engaged the California Model in a riveting conversation. I try for many minutes to convince her to kiss me. "Obviously that cannot happen because I'm very much in love with my boyfriend", she says. And then we did kiss. And it was not just a simple smack on the lips. It was an intense full-blown, sloppy wet kiss. When it ended, we both looked at each other with a "what the fuck, holy shit, that was amazing" grin. And then we immediately sprinted away from each other as fast as we could, and no one, not even us, ever brought it up again. Thank the Universe, there were no consequences and California Model, if you ever read this book, I hope you find this to be a courteous and respectful way of telling this story. Afterall, I will say to you here that I was an asshole and a jerk. I don't regret it, though, because that was my first wet kiss, so thank you. Still, please accept my apology: I'm sorry.

In the last year of high school, one of the students with very wealthy parents held a party. I felt very fortunate to be invited, considering my shenanigans. I completed the usual Zima ritual, and I'm pretty certain it was before midnight when I exited the party to make my way to the sleeping bag. In the morning there was a vibration of hullabaloo in the house. I woke up to an empty room which was odd because the room had twin beds and one was to be occupied by Lisa and the other by Keri. I was to be camped out in my sleeping bag on the floor. I rose, went downstairs to the kitchen to learn of some horrible news that one of the females had been assaulted sexually by one of the males who actually was sitting in a police car, handcuffed and everything. To be honest with you Dear Reader, I don't really remember many of the details of what occurred and if I did would not care to offer them here. It can lay dormant in 1999 and whoever it was that was assaulted, I hope that you have found peace and that you are prosperous.

Next, our high school principal completed an investigation in parallel with the local Macomb County police. Of course, having been at the party, I was interrogated. For the sake of the story, let's say the High School Principal is named Sam.

Sam sat me down in his office and began the interrogation.

Mike, this is a super big deal. Someone was physically assaulted. Do you know who?

I have no idea.

How can you possibly have no idea?

I was asleep by midnight.

This party went way into the night, and the assault happened around 3 AM. How are you sleeping by midnight?

In a very sarcastic tone (and I was also thinking: why also are you revealing a key detail regarding *when* – dumbass)

Because I went to bed.

Don't take that tone with me young man.

Then ask smarter questions.

He became enraged. His dull, white and freckled face turned merlot.

Okay smartass. Did you drink any alcohol at the party?

Yes.

Was it at the party?

Yes, I drank at the party. But if the question was, was the alcohol supplied by the party, then no, I brought my own.

Brought your own? You're 17. How in the heck were you able to bring your own and what did you bring?

I smiled with a huge shit-eating grin

Zima. I buy it from the Buscemis Pizza place not more than a mile from my house. They don't card me there because they think I'm 21. I never bring anything for anyone else if that's going to be your next dumb question. I always only ever bring a six-pack of Zima for myself, with my sleeping bag. So, if you've put it together, I drank my Zima and passed the fuck out by midnight in my sleeping bag which is why I don't know shit about shit. Anything else?

Yes, actually. Was anyone sleeping in the room with you and did you have sex with anyone?

When I went to the room and wrapped myself in the sleeping bag, no one else was in the room. The two twin beds, per pre-party plan, were to be occupied by Lisa and Keri. I don't actually know if they made it to the room because when I woke up, I was the only one in the room. I definitely did not have sex with anyone.

Sam, nonchalantly…

You're expelled for three days. I'll be giving your parents a call post haste. Get the hell out of my office; you should be ashamed of yourself.

I'm not, though. You know, all over the rest of the world it's not a big deal when you drink before you're twenty-one years old. Just sayin'. Having dinner with my 100% Italian Grandma (my mom), we share a glass of wine every night. You're the one who should be ashamed that you think I'm having any sex with anyone. Afterall my parents have conditioned me "to keep it in your pants, don't cha know, otherwise you'll burn, yah, in the fiery pits of hell".

Silence. I walked out of the office, meandered my way to my 1982 Ford Escort and drove myself home.

When I entered the door of my home, my dad and his wife were standing in front of the door with their arms folded across their chests and they were scowling. My dad is the only one who spoke.

You're a fucking embarrassment. How dare you do the Delitala namesake this egregious act of drinking and fornicating. You're grounded for the whole year. No TV. No parties. You'll be home promptly after school or work. We'll still let you play sports. But you better not fuck up your grades out of retaliation. I have to go talk to some young girl's father now about what you did to her.

I put it together quickly and probably because of the nonchalant way I answered to Sam, that Sam had really fucked me here. I interrupted my dad mid-sentence out of annoyance.

Stop! Drinking happened, that's correct. I did not have sex with Lisa or anyone that night. In fact, I've never had sex yet. You and all your talk about the fires of hell and shit, and I don't even make any attempts to date anyone.

Sam, that mother fucker, had told my parents that I had had sex with Lisa along with drinking when he called them to announce my expulsion. Lisa and I both denied it because it hadn't happened. And for real, if I had had sex with Lisa, I probably would have been fucking proud of it and then also admitted it because she was one of the cutest and sweetest. Since this probably won't make it into a subsequent chapter, I'll just let you know right now, Dear Reader, that I actually lost my virginity to a girl named Bernadette at the age of 19, and in the middle of a Canadian strip club and that is no fucking revision right there.

Because my dad didn't believe me, being grounded for one year remained the actual punishment. I rebelled in the only two ways I could. Number 1: I never once spoke one word to my dad or his wife for the entirety of the year. Not "hello", not "goodbye". When prompted, such as, "how was your day today, son?". I would honor that he had asked the question and acknowledge him with a nod or gesture out of respect, but I remained silent. Number 2 is a detail I'm not yet ready to reveal.

I had not been to any of the proms, but that senior year, I decided to go. I learned that Lisa did not yet have a date, and since everyone thought we were a *thing*, I decided to ask her out. By the way, she was way more popular than me, and she was way out of my league. What the fuck, classmates, you really think someone like Lisa would have been into this dude, seriously!

I asked her out to the prom because I thought it was a chivalrous thing to do and I think I also had a strategy to demonstrate, that by going to the dance together, we would prove that we were not actually together. I know that sounds confusing, but hear me out. At the dance, everyone would see us arrive, and they would be like, "see!" or "I knew it", but no one would ever see us dance, hold hands, or even kiss. Actually, Lisa and I even made an agreement that we are "just going as friends, dude". I, of course agreed to her terms immediately. By the way, I know what you're thinking, but *you were grounded.* I didn't give a shit. I went full out and used every single dollar I had saved from working at Ponderosa, rented a nice tux, rented us a limo, bought the corsage, and did my very best to show Lisa a G-rated good time. ("always be a gentleman").

The Lisa-Parental Units were super cool. Her dad knew her daughter, and he knew that nothing happened between us. So, he was cool, shook my hand, actually gave me a wink of an eye, and thanked me for giving Lisa an opportunity to have a date at her last prom. He also casually said, "That Sam is a real asshole, eh?". "Yes, sir", was my honest reply.

Anyway, we took a lot of pictures. An excessive amount of pictures, considering we were just friends. We went to the dance. We went to the afterparty. And that's when Lisa departed to find a different dude, and Jenny decided to find me. Me, still thinking I needed to be a gentleman for Lisa, plus scared of the fiery pits of hell, I just had a nice mind fuck of a conversation all night with Jenny.

One thing before we move onto Number 2.

Fuck you, Sam! How dare you, with your Christian set of values, tell two lies to two families. I didn't speak a word to my family after your lie for an entire year because they believed your stupid ass over me. You could have totally done the same thing with Lisa's family, and that is totally unacceptable. I hope it gives you night terrors, and since you believe in hell, I hope you fucking rot in it.

The second thing I did was that when I turned 18, I enlisted in the U.S. Army, and two weeks after graduating high school, I was shipped to Fort Lost in the Woods, Missouri, to begin basic combat training and become government property (G.I. = Government Issued in case you don't know).

On the day that I was to be shipped, I finally spoke to my dad. I was professional.

Dad, today I'm leaving your home. I've enlisted in the U.S. Army. I'll be training to be a Combat Medic, a 91B (articulated as a "ninety-one bravo"). Maybe I'll call home when we get the opportunity to do so. Maybe after all that I've demonstrated this year with straight-As, played varsity football, ran varsity track, and worked a job half-time, that maybe you'll believe me that I did not have sex with Lisa and that actually I still have not had any sex, thank you very much.

I anticipated there would be some emotional outburst and I was prepared for everything except what actually happened. At first I saw my dad tense up. Heard him take a deep breath. Saw him relax.

Ok Mike. Actually, I think is probably going to be the best thing for you. I've been over here worried about your indication of wanting to go to college, but you picked a party college and even said you picked it because it was a party college. And I ain't paying for no god damn parties. So, this will be good for you. I encourage you to go ahead, and please call home when and if it is permitted. I've missed you as my son, and I've missed hearing your voice, but I have been very proud of you for all that you've accomplished. One piece of advice and you better god damn hear me right now: If it ain't worth marrying, then don't stick your dick in it!

We both shared a boisterous laugh. I believe we even hugged it out. I believe we even told each other, "I love you". For the rest of my life, I believe I mostly took my dad's advice, and maybe the only time my dick went somewhere with someone who was not worth marrying was with Bernadette, at the age of 19, at a strip club. *Mostly*.

While in Combat Basic Training, I called home often, and my dad and I had a lot of great conversations. I came home on leave at Christmas, and much to my surprise, and I think Dear Reader, you will find this hilarious, there was a framed prom picture of Lisa and I hanging in what used to be my bedroom. Are you fucking kidding me? That's the worst.

Also, on this leave, my dad's wife had arranged for someone, someone that I believed I was in love with, to meet me at the house. As I have mentioned, I played high school football, and we had high-school cheerleaders. And one in particular paid a lot of attention to me, and I reciprocated. Her name is Tonya. We were very good friends in high-school, and she wrote me many letters to help me get through military training. Weekly. I looked forward to them and wrote her back every week.

Not too long ago, we talked every day.
We always had a plethora of things to say.

Then, something happened that I cannot explain.
I assume life took over and got in the way.

Attempts were made to keep in touch.
But I suppose that life was just way too much.

Our friendship became make-believe.
"Tag you're it" on the answering machine.

The days have passed that have turned into years.
And your voice I would so desperately love to hear.

I called and left a message once upon a time.
That was so long ago and still no reply.

I'd only require a few seconds of your time.
It'd be like the days of old and worth the dime.

Your number is locked away in my mind.
Oh, but today's too busy, I'll call another time.

And so it goes the same for you.

Are you too busy to call me too?

And the cycle repeats again and again.

You were once my best, now you're my lost friend.

Chapter 2 – Tonya

For those that don't know, when you first enter the military, you get your "basic training". It's eight weeks long, or at least it was when I entered. After the first week, which really is "hell week", and after you build some rapport and trust with the drill sergeants, you are allowed a few privileges. You're allowed to write as many letters as you want (even though you must spend your own dollars for the stamps, and believe me, you're not making anything when you're a Private or a Private E-2, which is what I was).

After Basic Training, you move on to your Military Occupational Specialty (MOS) training. In my case, as a 91B combat medic, it was 12 weeks long at Fort Sam Houston, San Antonio, Texas.

For twenty weeks, Tonya and I talked once a week by phone, and we were pen pals. I always looked forward to getting her letters because she usually would have a new photo of herself printed out for me. The guys in my squad were like, "dude, is that your girl? Daammnnn!". I would reply back, "I think so, but I'm not actually sure". I'm laughing out loud right now thinking about that.

In high school, Tonya and I were close friends. This really has to be set up correctly with context, Dear Reader, so please bear with me here. Tonya, as part of her DNA, is wildly affectionate with those she trusts and is comfortable with. I bet if I ran into her today, she would embrace me for what my wife would view as an uncomfortable amount of time. As is Tonya's way, she would probably plant a kiss on my cheek as well. We had Spanish class together, and I was her "little Miguelito". We would flirt endlessly, and she was one of the most beautiful ladies in the class.

Dark features. Dark hair, dark brown and large, oval, endless eyes with long lashes. She always had a great tan, always smelled like heaven, and had the physique of a Malibu surfer babe. I was smitten by her.

Having Tonya suddenly arrive was a very pleasing surprise, and I had no idea that either my dad or his wife knew that she and I had been in touch. She ran to me; we embraced for eternity. It was ecstasy. She was there to join me for dinner with the family and the reality was that no one else existed. We spent hours catching up and flirting. Even though I was an elite athlete in high school, the basic training had significantly transformed me into something else, and her hands were free to roam, and she was glad to explore.

Tonya was attending the "party school" mentioned previously, and that was the real reason I had wanted to go to that college, so fuck you, Dad for that (Asshole!). And it had the program for what I thought I wanted to be which was something in Sports Medicine or something like that. My dad was right though, it was the right thing for me, so thank you, Dad (genuinely). Anyway, I had asked

Tonya if I could take her out to dinner while I was in town, and she immediately accepted. I took her to what I thought was a nice prime rib restaurant. It was known for its great customer service and side-table salad service. It had a great ambiance. It was going to be a romantic evening. She and I are both 19 years old at this moment.

In preparation for the date, I went to the Lakeside Mall. I learned actually a week ago that the Lakeside Mall closed but the doors remain open for any mall walkers. Anyway, I stopped by Zales Jewelers and because, as an Enlisted guy, I could not yet afford an engagement ring, I bought her a pretty, rose gold XO bracelet. The circumference of the bracelet was made up of X's and O's smushed together like how I hoped our lips would be. I had it all planned out. The "it" is obviously in reference to the rest of our lives together.

At dinner, Tonya could tell I was a little nervous. She quizzed: "Are you okay, hun?"

I hope you're having a really good time, Tonya. I do actually have a couple of things on my mind. Over the last twenty weeks, I feel like we've really gotten to know each other. I don't know how you feel, but I want you to know that I'm madly in love with you.

My heart was pounding in my chest, and its vibration was in my ear drums.

I love you! I got you this gift and I'm hoping you can view this as a placeholder. I can't afford an engagement ring right now, but maybe this can be a promise bracelet. Will you marry me someday?

I had told the waitstaff and the manager of the restaurant that this was going to be a special occasion and they should check on us only minimally so that our special event would not accidentally be interrupted. At this point, I was pining for an interruption because the silence at the table was eerie. Tonya had turned a different shade of olive. I just kept thinking: *shit shit shit shit shit shit, what do I do now?*

Tonya finally broke the silence.

My little Miguelito. I love you as well but I don't think it's quite at the same level as that which you just expressed. Listen. I don't want to lose you. You're one of the best people I know on the planet. You're so far away in the Army and I'm so proud of you. I'm in college. That's where my focus has to be. So…Let's make a deal.

Fuck.

Let's keep up with each other just as we have. Let's make a point to keep in touch, and write letters. Maybe every so often we can see each other and see if that fire is still ablaze. And if by the time we both turn thirty, and neither of us are married, then yes, I will marry you. I can't believe you got me this beautiful bracelet. It's an insanely romantic gesture and I love it. I'm keeping it.

And then she stood up. So, I did too. She hugged me. She put her hands to my face and kissed me on the lips like Europeans do.

Since we had driven separately, that was the end of the date for her. She made her way for the door, she did glance back, she did smile, and she did wave goodbye. I waved back, and because at 19, I was emotionally retarded I didn't know what I was supposed to do next.

I finished my steak. I went home. I was devastated.

And also, there was hope.

I just had to wait eleven years, and hopefully neither of us would be married.

That kiss haunted me and I felt its impact long after the event.

Tonya and I did keep in touch regularly and neither of us ever broached the subject of whether one or the other was seeing anyone. To be honest, I knew she was seeing someone just like I was. When you really think about that, I bet we kept each other a secret from any current significant other. Seriously, if a current significant other caught wind of our conversations which were endlessly flirtatious, well, that would be the end of that relationship.

Fast forward four years and I take my exit from the military, head back to Michigan to pursue a Sports Medicine Degree from Eastern Michigan University. I had the G.I. Bill to help with tuition, a bunch of savings from the four years that I'm in the military, but I also needed a job to pay the rent and bills over the long term. I landed a job as the closing Manager at a Local Sporting Good's Store. Things are good. I have college friends, local friends, and friends from work. I'm achieving at school and work.

I decided to throw a keg party and invited the aforementioned and also Tonya. Everyone's having a great time. Then still emotionally retarded Mike sees Tonya go off with Dirty-Dick Dave. I'm twenty-two years old and of course I have this ridiculous rule that if Tonya were to be with anyone that I am friends with, then there is no way no how we ever get together. I don't tell her that though but as far as I was concerned the party was over except that it wasn't. I decided to play a fun game. Let's see how many babes I could kiss at my party. It turns out the number was four. And the last one ended with someone desiring to have their virginity taken, which I obliged.

I'm all shame and guilt. Yes, Tonya and Girl Number Four made their own adult decisions. Still, I'm a relationship guy plus the fiery pits of hell and all that. It took years and therapy to realize none of that shit matters.

A few months later, Tonya invites me and a friend to a concert. It's a double date. Me paired with Tonya and Arrow, (yes, like the D.C. comic book hero!) a friend of mine from college, paired with Tonya's Babe Friend. We have a pre-party at Tonya's apartment and get shit faced before the event even starts. We go to the concert; everyone falls down drunk, and we get kicked out of the event. We were in the elevator to get to the parking lot to get to the car, again, all four of us falling down drunk in the elevator. I'm serious, no one can stand or brace themselves against the wall. Then, I acted out violently. I assaulted Tonya by grabbing her in a private place.

She and her friend both reacted appropriately by beating the shit out of me with their purse and fists. She and her friend raced to their car (which had my jacket and phone in it) and they swiftly departed.

I'm not a violent guy. My action was completely unacceptable. You can hate me. I have never even thought about that kind of violence since, and it was never a thought prior.

This should make sense, but Tonya and I never spoke another word to each other again. I was not given an opportunity to apologize, and it is one of my life's greatest regrets. Tonya – I'm regrettably sorry. Trust me when I tell you that the Universe reacted and put my life out of balance for my egregious act towards you. I hope my act did not impact you psychologically or emotionally, and I'd be open to a conversation to hear anything you might want to say to me.

Dear Reader, I hope you will continue to remain with me, and I will understand if you do not. Please trust that this story does not end as one might anticipate.

When I feel like a tortured soul, poetry flows through the orbit of my skull. Around and around again through my eye sockets until I write it down. In case I'm not being clear, I literally see the words, and they don't go away until I record them. This is the poem that came to me after this sordid event:

Christmas was stolen on that night.

Everything should've gone wrong but instead went right.

We did double shots from a fifth of the Captain.
Not giving a damn about what might happen.

We thought we were in responsible hands
Not a single thought about life's reprimands.

So we got to the show and drank some more.
Danced and partied and fell on the floor.

We were complete idiots but got the laughs
But then our dates gave us the shaft.

They took off running through the gaits
We tried to follow up, but we had to urinate.

We arrived at the place where the dates had parked
But to our surprise, there was no more car.

And now the tension was starting to show.
They had our jackets and phones, and it was cold.

We waited on top of that structure
For what seemed at least an hour.

And you, my friend, passed out on the ground
And still our dates were nowhere to be found.

In fact, only ten cars still remained.
The situation growing tense and insane.

I approached some cars in quiet desperation.
Hoping some friendly face would take us to our destination.

Who had I become? Even my poetry was a lie!

That friendly face did appear though. I picked my friend up off the ground, fireman carried him to a car full of women where I desperately pleaded to please give us a ride to where we thought Tonya's apartment was. They had a better idea. The woman behind the wheel says, "just pile on in here, we'll take you back to our place and we can work out the rest of the details from there".

What choice did we have? I had asked for help and here it was. Another synchronous moment!

What could go wrong?

Technically speaking, I was in a five-some that night. Arrow and I are driven from the show to who-knows-who's house. I had already forgotten her name (shit shit shit shit shit what do I do now). The Alpha-Female invites us all to her bedroom. Like an Anne Rice Vampire, I hold out my hands, palms up, gesturing "come to me" and I even said, "I want this one". And so it was. Arrow was being occupied by the other two.

I was a lesbian that night. I made out with Alpha-Female and proceeded to scissor with her. She is all moan and groaning and "how do you know how to do that?". I didn't know that I knew how to do that. This night ends with the five of us in bed, with an Alpha-Female climax and an Arrow climax. Just to be clear, the bed was big enough that we had our own sections. Me and Alpha-Female. Arrow and his two.

The morning was extremely awkward when I learned that the Alpha-Female, who happens to be an ex-body-building-babe, is twenty years my senior and has a son my age. Eh, we decided to exchange numbers and give it a go. The other ladies had left already, so Alpha-Female drove us to where we should have been in the first place. There, Arrow and I see our jackets and phones in the parking lot, shredded and demolished as expected.

Alpha-Female and I spend a few weeks together, and we have a lot of intercourse. Her being twenty years older than me making the physical interaction excellent! I'm learning a lot of new tips and tricks that I had not been previously aware of. When she was *done,* her favorite way to end was to slide off and then give me a blow job. Remember, Dear Reader, I'm a relationship guy, and in these moments, I was so psychologically broken that I refused my own climax. Plus, "don't stick your dick in it" and the "fiery pits of hell". Towards the end of the second or third week of this I'm looking for my exit strategy because "always be a gentleman" and I'm so emotionally immature, I don't know how to break up with anyone. I didn't want to hurt her feelings. We wake up together one morning and she proceeds to get onto my computer and AOL chat with someone. I start a conversation.

Hey, who's that?

My girlfriend, but it's not what you think.

Uh, ok, can you explain it to me?

It's companionship.

For me, this does not morally compute, and I now have my exit strategy. I break it off with her and for several weeks she stalks me to have more sex but specifically to give me more blow jobs. I know to most 20-year-old dudes, it's like "yeah, bring that on please" plus also "Uh, she has a girlfriend, so there's a possibility of a threesome". For me, it was against all my personal moral standards. And I just want to be very clear. She was an amazing woman who had overcome an abusive relationship, and she had divorced her husband and raised two kids to be excellent kids (even though they were my age). She did not deserve this punk-ass behavior of mine. She was vulnerable with me. I was not able to reciprocate emotionally.

An emotionally mature Mike, the Revisionist writing this story, might have considered the opportunity to understand what she meant by "companionship". Back then, I had thought it must mean something physical, and also between two women, which was not something my upbringing had allowed me to accept. An emotionally mature Mike, after life experiences, may have found that to be worth more of his time to understand "companionship" plus the potential threesome, wink-wink, which she actually eluded to when we had the above conversation. Shit.

For her, I'm sure the experience was torture.

Specifically, that she was not able to get me to complete the act.

An act most men are known for completing in their very hurried way!

Intermission 2° *My Life Story* – Little Mike circa 1993

I was born, and then the family was torn.
When my mom gave birth, she suddenly went berserk.

I asked my dad. He said he was sad.
I figured it was all my fault that my mom was now in a vault.

My dad remarried, and that was good. We had someone around
to cook our food.
I remember things being good for a little while. Things were
great, I even smiled.

I have no brothers or sisters. Everything is on me. I feel like a
blister.
I feel like a blister waiting to be popped. The insanity is growing,
and it cannot be stopped.

I feel like the earth is crumbling around me. I'm so sick and
tired of my parents dumping on me.
They set all of these rules and regulations. I try hard to live up to
expectations.

I'm not happy at home, you see. I'm happy when friends gather
around me.

Everyone in my house is grumpy or angry. Hardly anyone is ever happy.

I try so hard to live by their rules. I'm sick of trying, I have to move.
My dad is cool, so my friends say, but lately he's been irate.
When I'm around them, I try to act right. No matter what happens, nothing is right.

Either it's my hair or the wrong look. I can't help that I'm not perfect!

I'm 16 now and I have a car. It's a shame they won't let me take it far.
I pay for everything you see, and that teaches me responsibility, I say sarcastically.

In reality, I'm a fake, and I try to fit into every clique.
I'm everyone else and not myself, Oh Universe, I really need some help.

If only my parents would let me be the kind of person I want to be.

I bet I would turn out to be pretty good if and only if they let me out from under the hood.

Maybe it's not their fault, maybe it's all mine. Maybe they're in their right mind.

Oh, Universe, I ask you this day, please, please! Show me the way!

And now that you are all snoring, thanks for reading my life story.

Chapter 3 – Laura

Dear Reader, I started this Volume of The Revisionist shortly after I had completed Volume 1, and in fact, Volume 1 was not yet technically published. For years, I have mentioned to close friends that I have an anthology of poetry. Poetry only ever comes to me when I feel tortured emotionally. I write this Volume not feeling tortured. That said, the poetry remains vivid and still serves as a record of the love found and the love lost. While I was combing through the anthology, I found a sequel to "My Life Story" from above, except that it was not poetry, and it was prose. I was delighted to be reminded of a story I had long forgotten. My Life Story II has an entry for Laura.

How could I ever forget "Little Laura"? Much like Tonya, I met Laura in high school. Again, like Tonya, we were in the same Spanish classes and even ran Track together. I was pretty blind in high school, and I did not know that Laura had a deep attraction to me. Believe me, the feeling was more than mutual. I am one of those people who fall in love at first sight, and with Laura, it was no different. In high school, one time, at a pep-rally, Little Laura walked up to me with a package in her hand that was covered in little hearts. It seriously reminded me of Nirvana's song, "Heart Shaped Box". Anyway, I was shocked to have this package in my hand and did not open it until I was home later in the evening. My senior prom was a bust for me. I went with a hot little number named Lisa. She was very sexy, and our prom outfits matched perfectly.

At the prom, Laura asked me for a dance. While we were dancing, she repeatedly told me how sexy I looked and, throughout the course of the prom event, asked me many times to dance with her, and I obliged her each time. She looked absolutely gorgeous, and the date that had brought her had only one thing on his mind that apparently Little Laura had on her mind with me. Out of nowhere comes a flash of light that on the dark dance floor blinded us for a few seconds. It ended up being an eternal attribute for Laura and me. The flash of light was of course, a photograph by the school photographer. This photograph, taken without our consent, ended up making one of the primary photos regarding prom and landed in the yearbook. It is what was in the box with the little hearts all over it. What an insanely romantic gesture. If you're wondering why I waited to open the box, it's because I was sitting next to Tonya at the time. (gasp)

If there is any such thing as "picture perfect", it was this picture that Laura had just given to me. We were embraced tightly, her pale cheek pressed firmly against my tanned cheek. We looked radiant together. She had even taken precious time and money to have the picture framed and formatted with a border that accented our happiness. When I told Tonya about it, all she could say was, "She really likes you Mike". I was without words.

A few months later, I was Army-bound. She and I kept in touch with an occasional letter, which was the initiation of some kind of relationship. The evening after my foolish performance with Tonya, I received a phone call from Little Laura. She wanted to meet me for a cup of Jo, and since my trip home had turned into something of a nightmare, I said "yes" because I wanted the trip to end on a good note. We went to this little coffee shop and had breakfast and a delightful conversation. It may have been the highest moment of the trip, and yet that's not completely fair, given the night with Tonya. I have to add to the story here that, quite unexpectedly, I caught Laura giving me an "I'm so interested in you" look. I told her right on the spot that I caught her and we had an irresistible laugh over it. We parted that day with hugs, and the next day I was on my way back to Maryland.

A few days later, I received a phone call from Laura. The conversation was still there and so were all of the irresistible laughs. Then Laura called me everyday, and just like that, we were dating. Even though we were miles away from each other, we were in love, and it felt amazing. I was able to visit her one time before the noticeable pattern of my life advanced its way to the late stage. I drove to see her from Maryland to Michigan and so our time was very limited together. We spent a few hours together in the evening and at dinner. We shared one beautiful and haunting kiss. It was a kiss where lips press and overlap; sensual, not sexual. It was a kiss good night as I had to make my way back to Maryland.

This cycle of conversation continues for a few months. Then Little Laura goes on spring break and cheats on me. The use of the word "cheating" is a bit aggressive. She had kissed some dude; they were both drunk. That's what happens on spring break but I actually would not know that since I was not ever allowed to go. Whatever. Of course, I broke up with her.

Laura and I only ever spoke once more. It's five years later. I'm living in Michigan again pursuing a degree. As arranged, I stopped by her home. I wanted to see how things "were". It's difficult to explain this. I wanted to see if she and I still had anything. "Anything" equates to emotions for each other, and "anything" also equals something to reconcile. Apparently, we did not on both accounts because I spent my time at her house jumping up and down on the trampoline with her little sister. Cased closed, Life goes on.

I was twenty-three when I wrote that, Dear Reader. The rest of the story of "My Life Story II" is written as a memoir that I generated to serve as my suicide note. Not just a suicide note, as the second title of the memoir informs me, a "Successful Suicide". I had made an attempt once when I was ten or eleven years old hence the adjective descriptor of "successful". At ten or eleven I was already hitting puberty and things are very bad in all areas of life which you know if you read Volume 1.

I found razors. I sit in the bathtub. Everything is very matter-of-fact. I have a plan. I've done the research and I know where to strike. I strike the place on my right arm. Blood is flowing into the tub. A lot of blood. Then, I started to notice this feeling come over me. The only way for me to describe this feeling is that I feel like my life force is flowing out of me. That feeling makes me panic. I do not want my lifeforce to leave me. I say it out loud to the Universe, although the Universe and I are not yet acquainted. I stand up, get out of the tub, wrap my arm in a towel and compress the wound. It takes a while but the bleeding stops. I am able to find a first aid kit and use the gauze pads. I stapled the wound just in case. As this attempt occurs in my dad's house, obviously the next step is clean up. I cleaned the tub. I did the laundry. There is not a shred of evidence for me to be caught except for the healing wound on my arm. The next day I have an indoor soccer game to play. I'm a forward wearing a T-shirt. And now Dear Reader, here comes the fucking punch line:

NOBODY EVER FUCKING NOTICED! (this is a serious *are you fucking kidding me* moment!)

Now you have the context for the working title. Speaking of context, there is more to provide. Before we move on from Little Laura though, the twenty-three-year-old version of me writes something compelling. The noticeable pattern of falling in love at first sight. The noticeable pattern of my life advancing its way to its late stage.

Intermission 3° *Ten Seconds* – Authored 08/09/2003

Ten seconds. The time it took for me to fall for you.
Would you believe that? I wouldn't expect you to.

You extended your elegant arm. Placed your hand inside mine.
I heard you say your name, but I was already blind.

I felt my jaw drop to the floor. What was going on?
I gave your hand a shake and released my hold, was that an
instant bond?

I took a step back and walked away as I heard everyone laugh.
I had to recompose myself. My head was spinning fast.

I sat down on the bed, placed my hands on my face, and felt a
rising warmth.
In my stomach, suddenly, there was a butterfly swarm.

I felt the prison chains release, the ones around my heart.
They had been there for so long and were too quick to depart.

I walked back out to see you, to see if I could speak.
But with raspy breath and deflated lungs, I spoke
incomprehensibly.

I've relived that moment a few hundred times where I was
blasted by your electricity.
A simple touch, a look into your eyes, Utopia and tranquility.

Will any more seconds be wasted away? Should we even keep
track?
Eighty-six thousand, four hundred in a day, but I want ten more
of them back.

One more to say the right thing. One for a longing gaze.
One to peak your intrigue. And one to clear the haze.

One to calm the storm brewing from inside.
One to stand in front of you instead of running to hide.

One more to measure what was going through your mind.
One for the connection to last for all time.

One more to appreciate the satiable rush.
The last to let linger; the uninhibited blush.

And for how long did it take for these feelings to swell?
Ten seconds to meet you…within ten, I fell.

Chapter 4 – Melisa

A fascinating concept about Army barracks life is the continuous arrivals and departures of personnel. Remaining for four years in one enlistment at the same base may have allowed me access to the comings and goings of nearly five thousand individuals. After graduating MOS training, and because I excelled in basic training and MOS training, I was recruited to be a laboratory technician at the Ft. Detrick, United States Army Medical Research Institute of Infectious Diseases (USAMRIID, or "RIID" for shorthand). You might recognize that acronym, Dear Reader, from the movie starring Dustin Hoffman, Renee Russo, and Morgan Freeman in "Outbreak". Adapted, of course, from the Richard Preston book, The Hotzone.

On a warm, sunny day in February 1996, I arrived, with several other new Privates, at the base and began the check-in process. We are promptly shipped to our barrack building, bags in hand, and on the front steps of the entrance, I see a beautiful blonde woman (and I know that you know what I'm going to say next, Dear Reader), and for me, it was love at first sight.

I dropped my bag. I didn't give a shit. I walked right up to her, gave her a penetrating gaze, held out my hand, and said, "Hi. I'm Mike Delitala. And you're the most beautiful woman I've seen in more than twenty weeks".

She smiled, revealing the cutest of dimples on her right cheek. Then she realized that I just caught her off guard. The smile vanished. She looked to the left nervously and then grabbed a long drag from her cigarette, deliberately blowing the smoke in my face. The look to the left was her involuntary glance to find her boyfriend, who at that very moment did take notice of me. He was a fairly large dude, approximately 6'4", of Spanish descent, and was rapidly making his way to confront me.

His trod turned into a sprint and he rushed me probably thinking he'd have an advantage given my short stature. To his surprise, I used his own momentum against him, and pile-drove him into the ground. A slight, surprised, gurgle escaped his esophagus. A second later, I was straddling him and delivered three gut punches and a right cross to his chin. Bap-bap-bap-boom! I didn't knock him out. He was, however, out of air. Then I choked him out the rest of the way until he was limp and lifeless. Since I was a recently trained combat medic, I checked his vitals, and he was alive and breathing. There were many witnesses to the entire thing, and calmly and coolly, I stood up, announced myself, and said, "Does this kind of thing happen a lot around here?" It was as if gravity were no longer a planetary concept with all of the slack jaws.

I stayed with him until he came too. And like old friends, we hugged it out, shook hands, and made our apologies. Obviously, I did not know they were together, and we could have just had words.

With that, he walked me over to this girlfriend and introduced me. Her name was Melisa. (That is the correct spelling in case you're wondering, Dear Reader). The dude then walked me to my room. It was another synchronous moment because, as it turned out, we were going to be roommates. Fuck my luck. And then a very delicious moment happened.

Melisa turns to the dude and says, "You're a fucking prick. I used you for sex. I fucking hate you. We're done".

She then turns to me in a sultry way and says, "You're coming with me. Let's go". And so I did.

She walks me to her room, and I'm feeling all kinds of shivers inside. Like, shit, are we about to have sex? Let me remind you Dear Reader, I haven't even unpacked my bags and I'm at my new home for not even 1 hour. Will it always be this exciting and adventurous?! Good grief! Anyway, besides shivers I'm having heart flutters. This is the most exciting and potentially erotic thing that has ever happened to me. Medieval even!

I enter her room. She sits me down on her barracks-issued love seat. We're sitting side by side and so I turn so that I don't have to turn my head to face her. She starts the conversation.

Wow. That was something. Look at you. Look at how fucking cute you are! You must not be more than 125lbs wet, and you just kicked my boyfriend's ass; well, ex-boyfriend now. He's known for fighting around here and also winning. In fact, he's never lost. And then you had the fucking nerve to be an actual medic after you handed his ass to him. Who does that? Shit, where are my manners? You want a beer or something? My name is Melisa. I've been here for one and a half years. I hold the rank of Specialist, and I work over in one of the labs in the main building.

It's very nice to meet you, Melisa. I mean, dude, he rushed me, I just reacted. Do you have anything stronger than a beer? I'm a gin and vodka kind of guy.

Melisa makes me a gin and tonic. It's been 20+ weeks since I've had anything to drink, and the warm buzz immediately sets in. I'm super comfortable. This is our first interaction together and it's so *easy*. It feels amazing. 10 seconds? And then, as it usually does, the 20-minute lull takes place. We find that we're each staring into each other's eyes. It's not uncomfortable. It's the most natural of things for us to be achieving in the moment. I go for it. I lean in, and we kiss passionately. It's fucking glorious and then, in typical emotionally retarded fashion, I run, in a sprint, out of the room. I imagine that Melisa laughed uncontrollably at my swift and unannounced departure.

In the event that the chronology feels off for you, Dear Reader, I'm 19 years old, and this is directly after the Tonya and Laura events. I'm not a virgin in this part of the story, but my only real experience is the Canadian strip club and, well, maybe one or two other experiences. That makes me laugh out loud, penning those words. I promptly return to my room, where I unpack and wonder if Dude will ever want a rematch, you know, perhaps in the middle of the night while I'm attempting to slumber in the bunk beds that we share.

I do not fall asleep that night. I'm all vibration and libido. I get up in the middle of the night, take myself to the shared-with-the-floor men's restroom, place myself on the John, and masturbate ferociously with Melisa in mind. She is of French ancestry, and her last name is shared with that of an expensive bottle of French wine. She has long, blond, curly hair that drapes perfectly with her chiseled triangle jawline leading to the perfect circle of her head. Her eyes are oval and change color based on her mood. They are mostly skyline blue. They drift to emerald when she's lost in her own thoughts, turned on right before intercourse, or taking long drags of her cigarette. She is long, lean, toned, and tan. And to top it off, she has a Devil tattoo on her left thigh that was stencilled in the ancient manner known as Tebori.(Tebori is a piercing technique. In her tattoo, they had pierced each point of the tattoo by dipping a needle in ink and then using a small hammer to pound the needle to puncture each mark into her thigh). It was extremely sexy, and she's obviously some kind of bad ass. She's twenty-five years old. That same night, well, it was morning now, I penned these words:

Shades of the Moon Authored MAR1999, Revised 2024

The moon is crimson tonight. Should I run away in fright?
Or should I bask in the rays of this blood light?

Is this how you feel tonight?

Maybe tomorrow it will be blue.
Are these the signs of how I feel towards you?
Maybe it's a sign of what I want to come true.
Maybe this is how you feel, too.

Then, the next day it might be black.
Suffering again from a love attack?
Sooner or later, all of this might crack.
And once more, I'll be flat on my back.

Blue, red, black, and white.
The different shades of the moon light.
I'll look at it every night.

To see if the moon feels like I might.
If so, I know it must be right.

A few weeks go by and I'm actively avoiding her. I'm embarrassed. She was never far away from my thoughts though, and the thought of the kiss, the passion of it, forced blood to an engorged hard-on every single time. (Raging fucking hormones etc.…Hurry, back to the John…) That said, barracks life is also party life. Inevitably, on any given night, in a barrack building that has three floors, two individuals sharing a room, times 30 rooms per floor, and it is 100% guaranteed there is a party somewhere. This party was in Melisa's room. She had tracked me down (finally) and said, "I'm throwing a party tonight, and I want you." She paused for dramatic effect, gauged my postural response, and then repeated the sentence with a slight addition. "I'm throwing a party tonight, and I want you to be there".She had smiled delicately, watching my reaction to her and she also had her confirmation that I also wanted her. Err, had wanted to attend the party.

I had made a couple of dude friends at this point. I'm brand new to the world basically, and they're slightly older than me so I start a very long system of inquiry as to *what do I do if* and *what happens if this happens* and so on and so forth. They're patient with me, but they also make fun of me a lot. Rightfully so. I didn't even have control over my own checkbook as of this moment, Dear Reader. I'm young and naïve, and I don't know what Melisa ever saw in me. Anyway, I arrive at the party with my dude friends.We're having a riotous good time. Everyone is getting along. I note that Dude is not at the party so I'm feeling relaxed and just being in the moment. We're all very drunk.

Suddenly, washing machine water from the laundry room next door floods Melisa's room. It's a torrential side-pour. Everyone is hysterically laughing including me. I'm laughing so hard that tears are coming out of both eyes. Melisa was some kind of upset, regained her composure, pointed at me with an arm fully extended like her index finger was, and said, "Well, I'm not dealing with this shit. I'm staying with you tonight". Of course, I did not disagree, and we made wild, passionate love all night long. I do mean all night. I had had the wherewithal to ask her if this would be "safe"? As in, birth control, safe. And this question came to mind and out of my mouth upon entry inside of her, to which she softly whispered, "Come anywhere you want Michael". And so I did, immediately. It was the first time that had happened and I had had sex three times previously. She looks at me with confidence in her eyes, a steely gaze actually, and says, "Don't worry about it. I wanted it like that. And god you feel fucking amazing". And being nineteen, with 3% body fat and raging fucking hormones, within 10 minutes, I was ready to go again and so we went. I took very cautious steps to be slow, measured, and deliberate for round two. I kissed her fully everywhere and soon I found her rhythm. And for round two, we both came at the same time. The event was heart-pounding and rigorous and we lay their panting to catch our breath. I had not made my exit from her yet, and we both quivered. She then announces to me, "that's the first time I've ever had an orgasm". I'm shocked as shit and ask a dumbshit question: "So that's good, right"? She immediately questioned whether this was my first time. I say, "not my first time but actually, my first orgasm *with* someone too".We share a cigarette together and blissfully pass out.

While in the military, I did not write one single poem other than the one above. I had found this amazing woman who was outgoing, wise, intelligent, had an amazing sense of humor, and was the sexiest woman on the base. We cultivated a friendship. Better said, we became best friends and loved each other's company. She made me more. In addition to our full-time jobs with the Army, I'm also attending a local community college, and I'm making rank very quickly. In fact, I was motivated to make rank quickly so that neither of us would have to have roommates. Once you reach the rank of Sergeant, E5, you get your own room. And after 2 years and 10 months of military experience, I graduated from the Primary Leadership and Development Course with honors and, just like that, was promoted immediately.

Having our fortress of solitude allowed us to make love every single night. And we did, too, and that's no Revision right there. Neither of us cared about the difference in age, and she was happy that I had a healthy amount of exploration within me. She told me once that she's not had this experience before. Most of the men she's been with before me were hurried and did not have so much passion. There was a slight twitch to my disposition at the mention of previous men, but I accepted the compliment.

My explorations were those of experimental proportions. In my own inner dialogue, "what happens if I run my fingertips just barely touching her skin all over her body?". Goosebumps turning into "take me from behind!". "What happens when I try a biting mouth massage all over her body". Moans and groans and "fuck my tits and then come on them!". You get the idea, Dear Reader. And so with Melisa, and over the course of our three years together, not only did I have a life time of exploration, but also some training. For example, she taught me best practices for going down on her. I loved it so it became part of the natural repertoire. She would return the favor, in the event that you're wondering.

Melisa is my first real and also long-term relationship. Melisa is one of the three women that I introduced to my dad (and his wife). However, my life is just getting started. Being a bit older than me, she has had life experience. My love for her, after about six months, starts to transition to something I can only label as "traditional". I'm suddenly jealous when she's interacting with other dudes, even though I already know that "outgoing" is her personality. I'm suddenly controlling in all of the wrong ways and I'm even demanding that she stop smoking cigarettes. I'm trying to change her into what I want versus what we have. At this moment in time, I also stopped listening and became what I like to call, Stubborn Asshole Mike (SAM). SAM can only see things SAM's way. SAM can only do things SAM's way, and no other way exists. Everyone else is wrong about everything and SAM is the only one who's smart enough to be right. This is real. SAM is universally angry even though SAM has exactly what he has been looking for. The Universe provided, SAM! (just sayin'). This is a direct result of my upbringing. I'm not mature enough to realize this, and Melisa is calm, patient, caring, and putting in all of the effort to keep the relationship, rather, the love for each other, real. I would wager that Melisa probably thought she could bring the version of Mike back from the first six months. I digress.

At about the three-year anniversary mark, Melisa and I begin engaging in plans for the future. The problem was that we were only having these discussions because obviously, this was the next milestone to hit. We both feel it. It is miserable with each other. Obviously in the way that I was raised, you grow up, you get married, and you have kids. And because Melisa has met my parents, because I have met hers, and because we're together, the next step is marriage. Some subtext for Melisa's parents. We went together to meet with them because I'm so traditional and chivalrous that I asked her dad for her hand. Her parents are top-secret, high-ranking, special forces, bad asses, and so her dad finds this to be quite comical. In fact, he ignored the request and looked at Melisa and said, "Really, this guy?". "Yeah dad, I love him, and he loves me, and we're amazing together", she says. He "grants" my request.

Of course I have our whole lives planned and figured out. The problem with that is never once did I include Melisa or invite her to share her ideas about our future together. "Traditional". I went to the local Zales. Purchased a 0.75c gold-band engagement ring. For an enlisted individual that's a very nice ring that is expensive to match. I reserved a table at the fanciest Italian restaurant in

Frederick, MD. We're enlisted soldiers living on an installation. We have never, not once before this moment, been on a date outside of the installation. Melisa is all calm. I'm a duck in water, but we have a good dinner. I'm not yet old enough to order myself an alcoholic drink. I had planned to ask her to marry me at the restaurant. Refer back to chapter 2 at my colossal fail with Tonya, and I decide at dinner that I need a backup plan. However, I don't really know anything about the area except that I remember passing a park on the way in.

I drive us to the park. It has a long walkway, and we begin to go for a walk. Melisa's growing irritable, and I can tell she's confused. It smells like goose shit, and in fact, the cement is covered in goose shit – everywhere. We're walking on it, in fact. In my mind, it's like, *it's now or never, dude!*

I get down on one knee (yes, in the goose shit!). I pull out the engagement ring, and I ask her to marry me. Tears of joy fill her emerald eyes, and she grabs my hand as a sign to stand up, we embrace for eternity and kiss sensually. I don't know if this is "yes", so dumbshit asks the question, "is that a 'yes'"? Emphatically, "Yes! Yes! That is a 'yes'!". Reflecting back on this, I had so much growing up to do in this moment.

Regarding our future. Melisa had 1.5 years left on her enlistment. I was ending my enlistment on 07/04/1999 with a Green to Gold scholarship, and Melisa was to join me in Michigan upon conclusion of her enlistment. The over and under on the amount of time we'd be apart in that scenario was a measly six months. Time flies: that's easy, except that we had never been apart for more than a few months while one or the other was in some kind of training or deployment. I had secured a very nice, large two-bedroom apartment for us in Ypsilanti, MI. I was also working full-time as a manager at a sporting goods store. Everything was going to be great. My spidey senses went off when I realized that we were no longer speaking to each other regularly on the phone. And just like that, she stopped taking my calls all together. I do not believe I have the vocabulary to articulate the dread and the anxiety that was blooming within me.

At the same time, what was I going to do? I'm in school full-time. I'm working full-time. I decided to dial a friend. I had had a falling out with my best friend and mentor so he was off the table for the call. You see, I had had sex with Melisa in a very public place, the cafeteria where we all ate, actually. And he thought he had finally caught us and was going to have our "asses involuntary separated" for our "lewd public acts". I'm laughing because Melisa and I used to have a lot of sex publicly and the only time we were caught was by local campers at the cliff of a mountain hike we used to hike regularly. They didn't seem to mind, and we didn't mind that they were watching.

I called Melisa's roommate. She declined to answer any questions. "Sorry dude, woman's code and shit". Fair enough. I called the only other person on the planet who I thought could advise the now twenty-two-year-old version of myself. This event precipitated our becoming best friends. For the sake of the story, we'll call him Montana (because that's where he's from and still lives today).

Montana answered the phone immediately with a high pitched, "MIIIIKKKKEEEE DEEEEEEEEEEEE!".

You see, I used to walk around the whole base screaming "MIKE D", and then pounce right into a Beastie Boys song, usually "Paul's Revere". Google the lyrics, Dear Reader, and this will make sense, I promise. I grew up with the cassette for their album "Ill Communication" and even at forty-seven years young, I can break out into rap with all the songs on the album and not miss a word.

I catch Montana up in exactly the way you are caught up, Dear Reader. And then…

Montana. I believe I've inherited a bit of clairvoyance from my Grandma. Dude, she used to be able to predict with uncanny fashion when someone was going to randomly show up at the house and want to have dinner with us. She'd say, "at such and such a time, so and so will be here. Yah, believe me, serious". And she was always right and I confirmed many times as an adult that there was no prior invitation. Seriously. Anyway, I have this very strange sense about something. I have this pervasive thought that Melisa has removed her engagement ring from her ring finger.

Can you do me a favor, Montana? You're friends with her too. Can you just check to see if I'm correct?

In his Montana drawl, he says, "well god damn Mike D! I had no idea. Man, that sucks. I thought you two were great with each other. Yeah of course. Let me go and see what's what".

I tell Montana The Revisionist's version of the next part of the story and he interrupts me mid-sentence.

Uh, no Mike D. No. That's not what happened next at all.

It isn't?

Nope.

Ok, I'm listening. Please help me remember this correctly.

First and foremost, I refused to be a middleman in this situation. I understood both perspectives very well. As you know, I'm friends with both of you. So, to make this an honest and fair deal, you have to talk to Melisa first and then you let me know when it's my time to do my part. I think that's fair.

Yeah man, except she's not taking my calls! It's all fucking too much and I feel like I'm taking crazy pills!! What the fuck am I supposed to do? I'm all the way in fucking Michigan with a full-time load in both school and work. This is not how it was supposed to fucking be, god damn it!

My voice is raised. My face is cabernet. My tears are torrential. And at some realization that actually all of these emotions and outbursts were futile, I suddenly go dark. Silent. Eerily. I sense that

Montana is getting uncomfortable. And then it's another fucking synchronous moment! Melisa calls and I break the silence.

Hey Montana – You're not going to believe this but she's calling me right now.

Rapid fire…

Hang in there brother. Try to take some deep breaths to center yourself. This might be your last chance to somehow try to reconcile this situation with her. You got this. Even if it doesn't turn out the way you want, just know you're going to be ok. I know for a god damn fact that you will be ok. You give me a call when you're done with that call.

Sure thing.

Click.

Dear Reader, before we move on to the Cross Over back to Melisa, Montana had also reminded me that I had sent him an email during this time with a poem pedantically titled, "I Want You, I Need You, I Miss You, I Love You". In searching for that poem in the anthology, I arrived at a handwritten outline on an aged and yellowed legal pad. That outline serves as the basis for the remainder of this chapter.

Hi Melisa – It's been a bit. I miss you so much! I know that you're probably going to break up with me. The last time we spoke, maybe a few months ago, you could not look me in the eye and you could not reciprocate with an "I love you, too". I think you mentioned you needed "some time and space".

Hi Michael. I miss you too. Frog has encouraged me to give you a call after the last time you called her to reach me. I thought, 'I'll give this one more shot'. Thank you for allowing me some time and space to just be in my thoughts. I do love you, you know.

"Time and space" took me back to her skyline blue eyes transitioning to emerald.

With a deep, long, and guttural sigh.

I needed to hear [the I love you]. Thank you. I love you so fucking much. I've been really confused. I don't know what's happening. I don't know why we stopped talking. I have this feeling of dread. That we might be over. I just can't stand the thought of that. Before you break up with me and hang up the phone and perhaps we never talk again, I just have a couple of things I've penned in front of me that I want to be sure are said, versus left unsaid. Would that be okay?

I didn't wait for her to respond and I launched into my agenda like a surprise attack.

I've come up with a list of reasons that I think we're breaking up:

1. Distance
2. My mood
3. [You] Found somebody else
4. My Move to Michigan
5. My dad (or his wife!) or my background

I could sense her irritation. Like, seriously, dude? I think for me, if I could get her to agree to one of the reasons, well, first of all, that would be something I could have as tangible and work on, and if not provided with that opportunity, then at least I could have some closure with a "real" reason. As it turns out, it was none of those. She reveals that the real reason is "that I don't know what I really want. It's always been this way, Michael. There has been this whole history about me that you have no clue about. I don't need to clue you in now, but, for example, I lost my virginity at thirteen, and I've probably had more than fifty partners, not including you. You're the longest I've ever been in a real relationship with. It scares the fuck out of me that this might actually be the last time I'm going to be with someone in this way".

I'm trying to find some chord of empathy in me but the reality is I'm all rage all of a sudden. *50 fucking dudes inside of you*, is one of my most prevalent thoughts and I almost vomit. I'm so disgusted. Afterall, she's number three or four, depending on a perspective.

I ask her a plethora of other futile questions, and she obliges with a response.

Why did you agree to marry me?

Simple, I loved you, and at the time you asked, I did want to marry you.

Why did you go to Pittsburgh to see me?

I knew in my heart that my mindset was shifting, and I wanted us to have one last and one more amazing go in the sack. It was beautiful, Michael; we made such passionate and rigorous love. You know you've broken me this way right? It will never be like this. This…This is unique to just you. Don't ever lose it.

From two weekends ago to this one weekend, what changed so suddenly?

I just. I. I just keep having this recurring dream about you, and when I wake up, I'm lonely.

Fuck.Ultimately, I'm realizing that my decision to exit the military, to grab an education, which was both of ours to make, and in support of each other is landing as the reason we lose each other.

I wax poetic for an eon on how I can be a better man for her and change.

Also, I've reached her. We're both crying and we have this urgent whine to our voices while we're each bumbling, stumbling, and trying to figure out the next "right" words. Dumbshit suddenly reemerges from his controlling and psychologically dependent trench where his insecurity is insurmountable, and he says, "I feel like you probably took your engagement ring off; you did, didn't you?".

Are you fucking kidding me right now? You just went on and on about how you can change. How can you be the man that you're meant to be for me? Like the man I met the first day you arrived at the base, all easy going, all laughs, and no deep spirals. You're not the man I fell in love with and I don't love who you've become. You're miserable. We're miserable together. But here's the deal: You left me. You're in Michigan. What am I supposed to do there? Have you fucking thought about that?

I'm bewildered.

No, Melisa. I have not thought about that.

Exactly. You've got this whole life planned for us, but you never even fucking once asked me about what I want to do.

It occurs to me, rather, I'm mindful of, that this seems to be the perfect opportunity to finally ask. It also occurs to me that I feel her growing more distant than ever before. Like the first day we met when she realized I had caught her off guard, and that dimpled smile vanished.

Melisa, what do you want to do?

Here's what I know. I've enjoyed our time together. God, I will never be able to forget you. You're a fucking force in this life and you have no idea who you are. I had hoped by now that you would grow the fuck up. I don't know. I think I must be holding you back somehow. I think this will have to happen in order for you to understand that you can't act in certain ways towards people. You're going to have to figure this out. I fucking hate that I'm going to break your heart. You need to know that my heart broke a few months ago when suddenly we're just no longer together. My soul hurts without you in my life.

Please. Melisa. Don't. Please don't. I want you. I need you. I miss you. I love you.

And as it turns out, I had penned her a poem with that title which suddenly burst into my mind and I read it to her. (Authored, 12MAR2000).

I want to feel you next to me when I wake in the morning.

I want to feel your warm body pressed against mine.

I want to kiss you sweetly to bring you out of your slumber.

I want to know that you're mine and no other.

I need to hear your voice each night before I sleep.

I need to touch your soft skin and play with your hair.

I need to feel your lips pressed against mine.

I need to know that I have you for all time.

I miss spending the whole day with you.

I miss not being able to see you every day.

I miss not being able to hear the words "I love you".

I miss looking into your eyes and knowing that it's true.

I love you for your style, class, and energy.

I love you for your intelligence, quick wits, and your beauty.

I love you for sharing your dreams and your fantasies.

But most of all, Love, I love you! When you love me.

This was not received as expected. I'm feeling her rage. I'm feeling that I should probably wrap this up.

Melisa, I want you to know that I have no regrets. You've given me closure here today with a reason that we are breaking up and I thank you for that and for taking the time. I have this feeling that I'll always love you and I really have no idea if that will turn out to be true. I have a few requests. Please read the letters that I've sent you. They will provide context that has been lacking from not being able to speak to each other for a bit. Maybe we can keep in touch? Also, please meet with Montana. I'd like to have the engagement ring back if you don't mind. It's quite expensive, and I'm in a bit of debt as a result. Since that ring was a promise, and the promise is broken, please give it to Montana. He's planning to bring it to me.

I was thinking I'd keep it.

That's really not the way it works. I'm sorry.

Ok then. I'll give it to Montana.

I'll aways love you; goodbye.

I hung up the phone. I grabbed a bottle of gin and fell in.

Melisa, of course, is an entry into the "Successful Suicide / Life Story II, so Dear Reader, I now offer you the prose of my twenty-four-year-old self:

I learned many skills while I was in the military. I became a phlebotomist, a medical laboratory technician, and then various other duties, such as the Training NCO, once I was promoted. I also met Melisa. She and I clicked instantaneously. As it turns out, I'm living in a Jerry Springer episode because her ex-boyfriend and I are roommates. That's not fucking awkward or anything! Anyway, she didn't really like him, but at the time, it had been a long time since she had sex, so she figured, why not? Then she met me, and there was an instant attraction. She was gorgeous. Long blonde hair, green eyes, muscular butt and legs, and even sexier than that was her personality. She was an outgoing, had a great sense of humor, and very intelligent and wise. She was, in effect, one of the guys.

We ended up being together for three years. The whole time we were together, we hardly ever separated except when either one of us had military training to go to or when it was time to go home and spend the holidays with relatives. During this whole time, I continued to excel in my career as well as advance my education at the local community college. To tell you the truth, I had never been so happy. I was important to the installation (everybody knew who I was), I was in college, and I was in the Army living an adventurous life, and I had someone (the woman of my dreams) to share it all with. So what happened?

I have a certain pattern in my life, it seems, and hopefully some day this pattern will dissolve. The pattern involves some type of relocation of my life. My four-year mark was rapidly on its way, and I knew I was getting out of the military. Melisa had only less than half of a year left and we discussed that she was going to get out so that we could start a life together. By this point, I had already proposed to her and we were planning our wedding and our future lives. So, I applied for and won an Active Duty Green to Gold scholarship in which the Army would pay for the college of my choice and the degree of my choice. I did this at our convenience. One less expense to worry about. I moved back to Michigan and not more than two months later, I was single again. She decided that she just could not be a part of the Michigan culture. Life goes on.

Unfortunately, I will be reminded of her for at least the next ten years. The engagement ring that I purchased was very expensive and I still own it today. All of the vacations she and I took are on the credit cards and since I no longer wish to be in the military, I have dropped my scholarship and owe the Army for one complete year of college. My total debt is $20,000. Yikes! It will take me at least ten years to pay all of that stuff off.

She lives in San Antonio, Texas and is still in the Army. We tried to become the friends we were before we made love that night, but it just didn't work. We had formed our pattern and we were stuck in it, never to be unstuck. She lost touch with me way before I considered giving up on her.

I also forgot to mention that I got us a really expensive apartment. I only wanted the best for us and I took her totally into consideration when I moved there, not me. What I am trying to convey is that because I had a shitty job coming out of the military getting ready for school, all of the money I had saved up I had to throw at the rent expense. It was all not very cool!

Anyway, I got over all of that: The lost job responsibility, lost love, lost friends, and loss of respect to start a completely fresh, new life. School started up again, and before too much time had elapsed, the Army, it, Melisa, quickly became a distant memory. I've done awesome in school. I'm currently maintaining a 3.75 GPA in one of the hardest curriculums that the school has to offer and I have been having fun doing it, too.

Twenty-four-year-old Mike identifies something profound in his attempt to explain to some imaginary reader as to why he's about to kill himself. There's that word again. "Pattern". Dear Reader, it is at this point, that I must remind you that, I am The Revisionist. How is the story progressing for you so far? Remember, this might not be real. It might, all of it, be the full truth. Again, I leave it up to you to make your own decision.

That said, at some point, The Editor is going to ask me, "What is this book actually about?". This book is about the noticeable patterns of our lives. For most of you on the planet, you are stuck in a pattern and you are also blind to it. Therefore, you are doomed to keep existing in that pattern, and for most of you, this will continue until you have your last breath, and you will believe that you are miserable. Or, you'll remain a victim and continue to blame everyone for all of the things that go wrong in your life. I promise you, Dear Reader, that there is a way out.

I'm not ready to reveal that to you. Breaking up inspired at least one poem, of course.

Either Way, Good or Bad – Authored 2000

Either Way, Good or Bad

I'll never forget the Times we had.

All the simple things, which make me smile.

All the time, you went the extra mile.

All the pleasures we hold so true.

Never forget, I'll always love you.

I am so sorry for the way I've been,

The jobs I've had have clogged my head.

In your heart, I hope you can see,

That I am trying to return to me.

The me you know and love so well

Not this other, a living hell.

The me that laughs at every joke,

Not the me that takes home my work.

The me that whispers in your ear,

Telling you, "I love you, dear."

And not for you, or because you say.

But because it is the only way,

For me to have a happy life

And hopefully, some day, to make you my wife.

And now this poem takes a different turn,

For there is something I want, need, and yearn.

The thing I yearn for is another chance,

To show you who I really am.

And either way, we both decide.

I'll still love you, keep you by my side.

Melisa, Dear, I love you so much

Please let us never lose touch.

There is so much more that I can say,

But one look in my eyes gives it away.

I wish not to end this poem,

Because just like our love, there is no end…

My going away gift from this installation was The Hotzone,

signed by all of the still-living characters of that true-to-life story,

and that's no fucking revision right there.

The ebbs and flows and fucking torture of love.

A love once lived. A love now lost. A life once lived. Because of love, now is lost. These are tragic words on that tragic day when love gets lost in its tragic way. It hurt more then. It still hurts now. Life goes on, some way, some how. Things change, and so do you. You changed us, and you changed me too. I changed, but not by choice. Words spoken unsaid or said. Either way, our love is dead. We both went on separate paths. It seems that choices are things that last! I know how I feel now. I remember how I felt then. Still, I need this moment to pretend to mend. Time heals, or so they say, but there's a reminder once a day. And then comes the torment of how we're not in our usual way. Still, friends we are. Still, friends we'll be. At the present, hopefully for eternity. It seems that I could drag this out. This story, how it broke out. But I feel that it's time to end. Time for head and heart to go and mend.

Chapter 5 – Veronica

Losing Melisa was devastating. I went into a deep depression. It was at this time that I discovered Trent Reznor and his band, Nine Inch Nails. I was listening to alternative rock in the early 2000s, and a song came on 89X, *the new rock alternative* radio station, and as I came to discover, the song was called "The Wretched". I was hooked. After work, I went to the local Meijer and purchased the double album "The Fragile". It would end up changing my musical interests, which, so far, has been my entire life. Anyway, "The Fragile" remains my favorite album of theirs and yes, Dear Reader, they still make music today. I guarantee you that in some form, method, or way, Nine Inch Nails has influenced you. I guarantee it! The Fragile is pure genius. It is dark. It is melodic. It is clever lyrically. And it was exactly what I needed to process the breakup with Melisa. I would come home from work, put the CD in the boom box, play it as loud as it could go without any distortion, and I would meditate to it as it played on repeat until I could fall asleep. I would become trance-like, put my chin to my chest, and just like that, the alarm would go off, and it was a new day. This went on for probably three months. By the way, Dear Reader, this body possesses two tattoos of something Nine Inch Nails related, and that's no fucking Revision right there!

At this point in the chronology of the story, I'm still newly departed from the military. I'm suffering psychologically, obviously. I'm in phenomenal shape. I'm also short and furry, and I'm significantly balding but not ready to accept it yet, and yes, I have a comb-over. Regarding being furry, it's robust. So much so that on my arms, chest, back, and full legs, the hair actually curled on itself. I guess the most important detail is that you couldn't actually see my skin through all of that hair. In other words, although I had a lot going for me, good looks were not one of those things. Also, I'm an "old-guy" compared to everyone else that I'm going to school with. I'm twenty-four.

For Veronica, Dear Reader, I've decided that you have to have the ending of the story before the beginning. You might hate me for that. Fuck you on this one. You'll understand in short order, and you might actually appreciate it.

And for the last time in this Volume, my twenty-four-year-old self:

Now, I bring you up to date on the current events of this life story. I turned 24 three days ago, and it was a pretty typical birthday for me. Only a few cards in the mail, a couple of emails, and one or two phone calls. Any gifts? No, just the ones that I went out and bought for myself. I bought myself a Power Tower and an abdominal machine. Well, at about 0400 in the morning, I heard the 'beep' of my cell phone. Of course that means I'm receiving a text message. There is only one person who texts me and that's Veronica. The message: "Do you still hate me? I miss talking to you". How profound.

Well, at that time of the morning, I was in no mood to reply so I waited until the afternoon some time. I met Veronica at my place of occupation, and just like any girl before her, it was love at fucking first sight. She walked past me with radiant youthfulness. She had long, dark brown hair, and it was fucking crazy curly and thick. Her legs were extremely sexy, and her dark brown eyes were shaped like almonds. Her lips were as full as her breasts, just gorgeous. My first impression was raised heart rates and the thought, 'damn, who is that!!' We hit if off immediately. The conversation came easy to us, which, as you already know from this story is a complete turn-on for me. Then, I was devastated to learn that she had a boyfriend already. Still, I couldn't help but notice the instant attraction between us; it was as if we already knew each other. She became impressed easily by my poetry as well as my muscles. Moaning slightly under her breath each time I let her touch me. Three days of heated flirting went on before we finally exchanged numbers. My balls turn blue. (Back to the John...) That night, she called me unexpectedly. We talk for hours, always reverting the conversation back to sex. She would say, "What would you do if I came over to your house and just started taking off my clothes?". I'd reply, "I'm a relationship guy, so you can strip if you want, and I'll fucking admire that beautiful body of yours, but nothing will happen between us if I don't feel something for you". Also, there is shock value in her statements which piques my interest and maybe "interest" can turn into "feeling something for her". Ultimately, this simple seduction won my heart.

A week later she invited herself to my place to "check her email". I set up an account for her on Hotmail because she claimed to not know how to do it. Of course, I failed to notice that she had brought an overnight bag with her. Suddenly, we're in my bedroom and she's seducing me with her eyes, her words, and her gorgeous figure.

She's telling me that I can rub her anywhere I want with clothes on or off and things of that nature. Now, this is three months later from the time that Melisa decided she did not want to live in Michigan, and so for me, it had been a while. I was getting turned on, but also I was frightened because of her intimidating beauty so, I ran out of the room. She pursued. She cornered me several times before our first kiss. We corner and kiss and corner and kiss a few more times before she said a phrase that I will never forget: Wanna fuck? I broke. We rushed to the bedroom where I gave her a ride that she would never forget. It was perfect.

There was the problem with her boyfriend though and I shouldn't even mention that she had another "buddy" on the side too. I laughed to myself silently as I figured I was just another toy for her. I'm not into one-night stands but I figured she got what she wanted and was done with me. It inspired me to write "Sorceress of Seduction" which I sent to her new email address that I had just recently created for her. Two weeks later we were making love on a regular basis and I feel like I'm losing my heart again. I made her decide between her boyfriend or me, but she couldn't have both. She chose me.

For six months we were stellar. We went places with each other, we made love, we did things together, we made love, just enjoyed everything about each other, and, of course, we made love. We made love more than any porn star or any springtime rabbit. We were perfect. Unfortunately, it became a problem because we also worked together. And she was so much younger than I that most of the time she was unable to separate our professional and personal lives. And because the store manager didn't want to give her a raise, she quit and started to work elsewhere. This place, this elsewhere started the downward trend that I like to call "us".

Suddenly, we weren't seeing each other ever. We barely spoke on the phone; we weren't making love anymore, yet we stayed together. And then I broke into the trend that I call my life. I started to not trust her because she didn't want to tell me the details of her life. It got so bad, that I was not even invited to go out with her and her newfound friends. I went from perfect boyfriend, sweet and caring, to paranoid, nontrusting, and interrogatory. The months went by. I had school to keep me busy as well as work, and she had the same. We were together just for the sake of saying we were, not to mention that we are both helpless romantics and let love guide us blindly. I lowered my expectations of the relationship and got to a place of not giving a damn. I lowered them so much that I only expected we should see each other on special occasions. You know, birthdays, Thanksgiving, anniversaries, days like that. Well, wouldn't you know, when one of those days came by, I'd at least hear from her but not until very late in the evening or sometimes not until it was the next day. I let this go on for a whole year until she did it to me again on Valentine's Day. And when I was ditched on Valentine's Day for some "friend problem", I had had enough, and I said goodbye.

Of course there was another event that happened in our lives that I have to mention because it will explain so much later on in the story when I reveal to you the very specific manner in which I will end my life. All of those times she and I made love, we never once, used protection. I don't wear condoms. She's not on any birth control because her parents won't let her and they think she's their little virgin daughter. This 19-year-old has had more partners than I have at this point! We relied on the luck of Mother Nature (that whoring bitch!) to keep us safe. Mother Nature became angry with us for the way we were treating each other and decided to give us a sense of urgency by blessing us with a child. Veronica was pregnant. The funny thing about it (if there can be anything funny about this) is that while we were making love, I knew the exact instant it happened and even said, "Oh shit" in the middle of it. It was the pre-come that did us in, not coming inside of her, although, she did allow that on occasion. I suggested a million times that she get herself tested so that we could decide how we were going to handle it. She absolutely refused. I suggested it so many times that finally she said, "Stop bothering me about it." So, that's exactly what I did and then she disappeared for a while again. Three months later, or so it seemed to me, she came strolling into the store where I worked, and my exact words were, "Hey, are you still my girlfriend?". To which she replied, "Yeah, I think so, do you not want me to be?". Then we took a walk through the store, and she told me she was pregnant. "I know. I've known for a long time". I then implied to her that I wanted to keep it. That was my first mistake. I only implied it. After I implied it, I never said anything again about it. Two weeks later, there we are sitting in an abortion clinic. She had the procedure done to her, but I was the one who looked like I was in pain. And just that quick, my kid was killed, and I never even had a choice in it. It was a true test of the difference between saying you're pro-choice and actually fucking being it. Unfortunately and regrettably, I passed that test. We only stayed together for two months after that. Remarkably, immediately following the procedure, we had sex. Veronica pulled out a condom. I put it on. We had sex. It was unremarkable except for all of her blood all over the condom. We may stay together for two more months. During those two months, we broke up and got back together repeatedly. It was pain (torturous), and it was love, and it was more pain (ebbs), and it was love again (flows).

Veronica and I were able to become friends for a few weeks after we broke up for the last time. We helped each other out through the painful process. We even talked about the abortion, something that was unutterable previously. She almost killed me when she said, "Mike, I never said anything because I was scared, but I wanted to keep the kid too." I was so shocked. The tears just came flying out of my face. I placed my hands on my head and just looked away. I had my exit strategy. We embraced for a very long time. We just held each other, possibly forgiving each other for such a mortal decision that was all knee-jerk reaction and devoid of critical thought. We got each other to laugh once more so that we could remember the other's smile for the following months and gave each other one last passionate kiss. I'll never forget it; I sure as hell didn't want her to leave.

I had planned on remaining a very close friend of hers but other curses found their way to me. I began to go on a drinking rampage. I went out with friends almost every night in search of a new girlfriend. I met a lot of girls who seemed very interested in me until they would ask me when the last time I had a girlfriend was and who she was. Of course, Mr. Integrity would answer honestly. Just another mistake because, as it turned out, every single girl I met had some kind of fucking connection to Veronica. Are you fucking kidding me? They would say that they were sorry and they couldn't date me because they were scared that Veronica would hunt them down and fucking murder them. After the tenth time it became all too ridiculous and more and more I started to hate her. Then, the last straw. I was at a party making significant progress with a blonde bombshell (BB). We were just about to kiss when I received one of those fucking anonymous "beeps." I wanted to ignore it but BB insists that we look at it together. She reads it over my shoulder with me and this is what it said: I bet you're picking up some cute blonde right now. Very true and very scary that she knew that. BB freaks out and runs out of the room in the same manner I had previously skedaddled with Melisa. Except, I never see her again.

Now I'm truly hating Veronica because I felt like I was being cock-blocked in the whole city of Ypsilanti. Not only that, but each time I came home from some club or some party, Veronica would call me just to say she knew where I was and whom I was with. I felt stalked, and I felt pissed off. I mean, I totally let her go and did not keep up in the slightest with her life, yet she continually knew where I was, who I was with, and what time I was getting home. Not only that, but I guess to get back at me (although this is only rumor), she slept with three of my close friends. I wish someone would tell me exactly how does something like that have any impact on me? I don't get that. It's simple, I just stop being friends with those fucks.

Then I realized the real reason I hated her. It wasn't because I was being cock-blocked or stalked or that she was sleeping with my friends, that's childish. It was because I could not bring myself to forgive her for killing my kid. I wonder what my future self will think of this. Random number…what will my forty-seven-year-old version of myself think. Shit, I'm planning my suicide right now. There will not be an older version of myself. Fuck myself! Not only killing my kid, but I let it fucking happen. I even put it on the fucking credit card! God damn it!

Then, I did something even more pedantic and sent her hate emails. I wrote a hate poem as a second edition to "Sorceress of Seduction" entitled "Seductress Revisited". I sent it to the email address that serves as the origin of this whole sordid story, expecting to receive a snarling response. I blocked her from sending me emails, told her to never call me again, to not text message me, basically to never contact me in any way. These are true signs of showing someone how much you love to hate them.

I went out with a very close friend who is a girl last night (Tonya – are you fucking kidding me!), and out of the blue, a month and a half later, telling Veronica a big F U, and here comes the inevitable text (deep fucking sigh). All I could do was laugh. I mean, it was as if her "Mike radar" went off and she needed to cock block me. You're getting cock! Why is it such a problem for me to use mine. Jesus H! It didn't spoil the mood (thank the stars!). "Do you still hate me? I miss talking to you". I was drunk and agreed to talk to her but I never did.

Go ahead Dear Reader, take a break. That was intense. It was intense for me to relive it.

Veronica is a force of life on this planet. Thinking about her and the 24-year-old version of myself, I can say that, yes, I'm still lacking in wisdom and smarts, yet I'm getting better at this thing called love and life. You realize of course, that this is the same story as Melisa and Mike, except Mike is Melisa and Veronica is Mike. She's brand new to the world with a system of inquiry for *what would happen when I do this* and *if you like it when I do this or that*.

I do grow insanely in love with her. I've grown up a little, though. Although it is love at first sight, I at least try to get to know her and befriend her before jumping head on with my emotions. This is progress. This is breaking the pattern. Notice the word "trend" in that story. Younger Mike is about to realize his patterns and younger Mike is, at least in thought, making strides in being introspective and trying to figure out how to not be in so much pain (torture) regarding love.

That first time that Veronica came over was both a mind fuck and an actual fuck. Veronica, by the way, holds the record for how many times I've fucked and came in a single night. The number is four. You're reading that correctly, Dear Reader. And I had mono. Veronica, by far, at least until I married, was the sexiest woman I've ever had the pleasure of (fill in the blank). Her skin was porcelain white, like an Anne Rice Vampire. You already know about her dark features. She was a long-distance runner and was nineteen. She had a Barbie body with 3% body fat. Except that she had the largest breasts I've ever had in my hands and mouth. The men in my family really liked to hug her inappropriately, thumbs in the side swell and everything (fucking gross, old, white guys). She asked to be titty fucked quite often. Shit, she loved it in all orifices. She was also a tad sadomasochist and loved to have her nipples bitten hard! (which made me really uncomfortable).

Listen, until you get to a certain age when you're a dude, you do worry about your dick size. Here was Veronica, at 19, already more sexually seasoned than me, and her boyfriend before me was a huge dude. To my knowledge, dudes who are larger, well, are larger everywhere. I didn't have stage fright, but knowing this put a little angst within me. Once her clothes were off, I sprung the largest boner I could possibly produce. She guided me in. Her eyes went into the back of her head as she uttered, "Oh my fucking god you're fucking huge." I didn't know that before that moment and it gave me the confidence to get her to have her first ever orgasm. She felt as though her power was taken away by the act of the climax and so it would be the first and the last, as I would like to say. I would check in on that topic every once in a while. You know, is there something more I could do for you? Is there any way you want me to be different? Just show me. She said she was 100% satisfied and to just "keep fucking me. I don't want to feel like a fucking housewife, treated all dainty and proper and shit".

Fair enough, it will be my absolute pleasure to continue to fuck you. And since we're still stuck on the first night, Dear Reader, here is the Sorceress of Seduction:

Sorceress of Seduction – Authored 26MAR2001

Sorceress of Seduction is the name that she takes.
Stealing your soul with pleasurable aches.

The pleasure arrives in its many forms.
First to your emotions, and then to your bones.

Dark, devilish hair, with black, inviting eyes.
Lean, long legs with strong, muscular thighs.

You end up hypnotized as she passes by.
Perfume and pheromones, and hips swinging side to side.

She uses her magic and her powers of lust,
to break down your will, to indulge in your trust.

She reaches out and touches your hand.
She soothingly says, "you will do as I command."

You do as she says, but you want to run.

The bad side wins when it's time for bad fun.

She grins a smile that only the devil can give.
Touches your face and gives you a kiss.

The kiss is sweet like none before.
You can't help but want more and more.

Her hands move down to touch bare chest.
Nothing feels better than flesh on flesh.

Then, a thought suddenly appears.
It's not too late to battle your fears.

There's still time for willpower to win.
But for you, it's too late, and you give in.

She still moves down and caresses your thighs.
Suddenly, you feel your heart rate rise.

Then, like the wind, she swoops you away.
Takes you to that place that I need not say.

When all is done, you lie on the bed
to count all of the fantasies strumming through your head.

Then she's gone. You're all alone.
No good-byes. Not even a note.

She leaves you this way so that you may know,
she was in charge, and you were just a show.

But before this tale can be completely told,
there are still some items that we need to unfold.

It seems that the Seductress will always win.
Temptation and desire make you always give in.

When she has had her way, and all is done,
Your heart will be empty, but it will be worth all of the fun!

Just so you know, Dear Reader. Veronica is living her best life with a wonderful husband and two lovely children in Michigan. We did end up getting back in touch, mostly through social media. With time I grew to understand all of our decisions relative to the lack of our options. And with the writing of this volume, we have planned that we will jump into a Zoom so that I can give her some options with how her chapter has landed. She has already reminded me, via a LinkedIn message, "that we very nearly destroyed each other." And she had a tantalizing thought about what I might say regarding her perspective. Stay tuned, Dear Reader, there might be a significant Revision about to take place. I feel this chapter must end right now and give you the sequel to "Sorceress of Seduction." Refer to Appendix 1 for a letter that I wrote to Veronica after our break up to try to bring us both some closure. It's not what you're expecting, Dear Reader, I promise!

Seductress Revisited

She has become a virus without a cure.
Always changing her structure to combat the treatment.

She is like the winter that will not give in to spring.
The sun shines through to tease, only to hide behind clouds to
bring cold and suffering.

She is the festering high-school injury.
The nagging excuse for not enjoying life.

She is the skipping record playing the same annoying lyric.
The repetitiveness of the same becomes typical of all that she is.

She is the Goddess of Lies and the Temptress of Evil.
Each new fabric of the story becomes interwoven into a fictitious
yet believable truth.

She is the scab that covers the in-grown facial hair.
The kind that brings blemish to every face of beauty.

Her lack of conscience equals her personality and her soullessness.

The simplicity of her negativity is proven with each vulgar word uttered.

She is the flickering light bulb that has not yet burnt out.

The constant on/off fluorescence desensitises eyes and causes migraines.

She is the upright, decaying tree with roots delved deep into the earth.

Blocking the path of the future with incognizant stubbornness.

She is the one and only...regret.

Chapter 5.1

In the in-between moments when Veronica and I were off again, there were a few intermediaries. A few blissful passersby if you will. I was visiting a mentor in Kentucky, and the same day that I arrived to his house, is the same night that I met Tamora. My mentor took me to a local pub so that we could do shots and get lit off of cheap beer. I see a cute, short, white, blonde babe, and by this time, I have my repertoire down. It's super simple. It's "Hi, I'm Mike," with my hand held out for a shake and a steely and yet friendly and also penetrating gaze in their eyes. If nothing else, it always strikes up a good conversation which is all I really care about in the first place. Remember, I am a relationship guy.

Hi, I'm Tamora. You are such a super cute dude. What makes you approach me tonight?

Shit. Here we go again. "What makes me approach you tonight? That is an excellent question Tamora". Except this time Dear Reader, it is NOT love at first sight. But, it is desire. I notice that something is not quite right but I do not pay attention to any of it. Her jeans are unintentionally perforated; in spots that are unflattering. Her shirt is dirty; dusty might be a more apt description. As for the rest of her she's flawless and her hygiene is up to my high standards or expectations based on your perception or preference. Her hair is nicely combed, and her nails are a pretty pink. She has on cheap perfume and I have this strange thought that I hope it is not covering up body odors emanating from where we all know they do. Tamora continues the conversation and in a sultry voice…

Listen Mike, it's very nice to meet you. It's really loud in here. Do you want to walk with me on the beach?

Absolutely. Let's get out of here.

I motioned to my mentor with an "okay" gesture and a "heading out" gesture, to which he gave me a thumbs up. We're good to go. He's busy looking for his kill anyway and doesn't give a shit. She grabs my hand to hold it and walks in front of me as we navigate away from all of the pub patrons. I notice that she's super fit, and I'm assuming she's in the military, the same base and probably the same platoon as my mentor. My heart is in my eardrums again. I'm pretty sure she could feel my heart rate jump through the wrist that she was holding because she turned my way, and whispered in my ear, "Calm down, Michael, I've got you". I was not calm. And I was already raging boner; one track mind and "oops, sorry to run into you, with, uh, that."

We made small talk on the beach. We sit on a bench together. It's lighted by an overhead lamp. We can see each very clearly now versus the darkness of the pub. We both like what we see. Our pupils are quarters. She asks if she can touch me. What she means is can she put her hands on my body? I nod. She begins to massage my shoulders, then triceps, works her way down to my biceps, transitions to my chest, pulls up and off my shirt, and then washes her hands on my chiseled abs. She's flustered and red in the face and is ooing and ohing with a rapid cadence to her breath. She says, "god, you look and feel like Superman". I chuckle to myself quietly because although I have a Batman tattoo, I certainly have never been compared to Superman by anyone. She then straddles me and is grinding herself on me while throwing her hair backward. It's one of the most erotic moments of my life because I know her name and nothing else and as I keep reminding you and myself, I'm a relationship guy (shit shit shit shit, what's going to happen next!). By this time, her shirt is also off and her front swells are colliding with my face and mouth. She announces to me, "no strings attached tonight, Michael, I promise. Let's just have fun and enjoy each other. To that end, may I please please please suck you off".

I didn't even have a chance to respond and the act was already in process. I have to admit, I was a bit concerned at this moment. This is not something that has ever happened to me before. I do not know this person. I'm suddenly wondering if someone is going to bash my head in from behind, leaving my lifeless body to be found by some random stranger. My thoughts also travel to *what if this woman is a serial killer* and, like a praying mantis, will rip my dick off after or slice my neck open. She notices my unease because I'm deflated a tad.

She comes up for air. Meets me at eye level. In a very caring and somewhat of a fevered pitch…

What's wrong Michael? Please, I want it all!

I explain.

Don't worry. This moment is meant for just the two of us. I need it. Give it to me.

And so I give in and I give it to her. In this instance it is actually the full act. It's the first time, that for this act, I go all in. You see, I enjoy watching this act in porn. I enjoy when a woman wants to take it all in. But, in reality, when I'm with someone, I find the full act to be discourteous and that it should not ever be imparted on someone unless they request it. "Always be a gentleman," and this act requires full consent from all involved and prior to the act; otherwise, you're a piece of shit. I'm twenty-five years old and still all raging hormones and 5% body fat, so I'm still ready to go and ask her if 1) I could return the favor and 2) if she'd like something else to be all in inside of her that is.

Michael, I have a confession to make.

Fuck. I knew it. Just like Admiral Ackbar in Star Wars, it's a trap!

I lied. The strings are attached now. I'm married. I'm married to a high-ranking individual on this base. But listen. He abuses me. I saw you in the pub. And you look so fucking strong, and I could tell just by your introduction that you are a sweet man who can help me and rescue me. I just swallowed you, and I know you'll do the right thing and help me. You'll help me, right Michael?

Are you fucking serious right now? A Mike just five years ago would have been Mr Obligation and would have accepted the offer. This version of Mike declined. Just like I'm declining to tell you the rest of that sordid story, Dear Reader. That night, it came to fisticuffs with her husband, who had been trying to locate her and then did, while her top was still off and other such signs of our *act*. I'm 4-0 when it comes to fights Dear Reader, and I took this abusive asshole of a husband right down to the wire of his disgusting life. And that's all I have to say about that. I impart a "goodbye" to Tamora, "thanks for the great and fucked up night. Obviously, you've got your work ahead of you to figure this out. When you figure it out…look me up. It's clear there is an amazing attraction between us. All of this, the whole thing, I don't *do* any of this". And then I ran away as fast as I could to get back to the Mentor's house.

About six years later, Tamora tracks me down to where I'm residing. I'm having a drink with Tonya at my apartment when the doorbell rings. There's no such thing as Ring at this time and I'm not expecting anyone, but I open the door regardless. She has the nerve to say, "Who the fuck is that on your couch?". Which, I then have to break up a fight between Tonya and Tamora. Tamora has taken on new and horrible characteristics. She has a meth mouth. And tracks. Jesus H! I send her away and tell her never to come back.

Writing all of this makes me feel terrible for her. As my wife would say though, "choices and consequences". Very true. Tamora does make me feel tortured when I learn that I may have been a homewrecker. I don't feel tortured by the act; instead tortured by the premise that I could have asked more questions. I could have paid attention more to the faint tan line on her wedding finger. Whatever. Life is a battlefield and we were both consenting adults. If there is a life lesson here, it's that this version of Mike was starting to understand the complexities of adult relationships. And I have to give it to my 25-year-old self: You finally learned to let go and let yourself be vulnerable and human. If I were talking to you today, I would tell you, "You're almost ready to finally actually be with someone". Almost.

I dove deep into the archives and found this untitled work. The electronic file notes this as "Tamora Poem", 19AUG2000.

I, myself have had so far a day of hope.... a day of dreams, and a day of warmth. I have rang my bells for many miles and stepped over the hill........not only see the truth but to feel it as well. I have felt the caress of the cat and her dress. I have felt the soft silk of satin that she holds and the velvet hat that she unfolds. But still, I turn to return. Here it is, the magic pot of gold. So it simmers of shine........but yet it is of mold. It is corroded of disaster, and hurt, remorse......but it is still remote for it is a pot of gold. A pot of gold that vanishes within your very eyes into only

mold. But I shall raise my head.......and feel not cold......but bold
for I am the true pot of gold.

I don't know what that means either. I hope you're laughing, Dear Reader. Moving on…

Intermission 6° NIGHTCLUB – Authored 09OCT2002, Revised 10SEP2024.

In this place, during this time,
Take a chance and stroll inside.

And once inside, you will see,
Accidents were done purposefully.

On the window, a fingerprint smudge.
Under the table, a flirtful nudge.

From the jukebox, a familiar song.
In the stall, a shredded thong.

On the floor, a broken tile.
In the corner, a gorgeous smile.

People dancing everywhere.
A casual flip of chestnut hair.

A high-five motion of slapping hands.
On the stage, a local band.
Vampire ladies sucking beer through straws.
Picture perfect, noting flaws.

Lines that flow into the hall.
A used condom in that stall.

Bladders that lack self-control.
Urinals that overflow.

Snowflakes falling from the sky.
Buzzing from a natural high.

Name heart name carved into wood.
Scarfing down some finger food.

Anticipation, nervous twitch.
Another damn computer glitch.

Twinkle, sparkle in the eye.
Another stupid pickup line.

Inhale, exhale, pheromones.
Ringing, buzzing, cellular phones.

Boy-girl games of fake charades.
Number exchange for future lays.

Door-to-door midnight crawl.
"Last chance for alcohol!"

Captain and Coke to ease the mind.
Bodies caught in the bump and grind.

Shitting, pissing, throwing up.
GOOD TIMES! @ The Nightclub.

Chapter 5.2

Like my stature, I'll keep this short. Bring in a number named Kate. To spare you the agony of redundancy, Dear Reader, I'll simply mention that Kate could be Veronica's doppelganger. In the chronology of events, Kate happens right after the final break up with Veronica and, if memory serves, in the same week. Imagine my state of mind. I was out for some revenge sex. I know that Kate has a long-term boyfriend, and she wears a promise ring to highlight that she is unavailable for the foreseeable future. Much like Veronica, Kate takes notice of me because of my confidence, swagger, and unapologetic disposition in constantly flirting with her and trying to get her to come home with me. She's nineteen and I'm twenty-five. I'm a disgusting individual in this chapter. I'm a borderline alcoholic. I might also be borderline. My moods swing like a pendulum. Whenever I think of Kate, even today, the Nine Inch Nails song "The Fragile" spins around in my head. I don't know why. My therapist and I are unable to figure this out, so we've moved on. I've placed the Lyrics of that song into Appendix 2 for your review. I think you should review it Dear Reader, before going any further into this Volume.

I finally convince Kate that she should give me a try before she enters the final volume of her tale and is married. She considers this because some friend of hers persuades her that Kate might not know what she really wants and to give that dude at work a try.

"Your boy-friend never needs to know and, especially if it convinces you that your boyfriend is actually the one". Kate invites me over to her house to meet her parents. I don't know why. Perhaps just to see if I was a good guy or not and could I get along with them. It was a test. I passed. Parents always love me because I'm "always being a gentleman."

The next day we have it all planned out. Kate is going to arrive at my apartment and then we'll just evaluate what to do from there. She bursts through my apartment door, her guns blazing. She told me later that she had to work up some kind of courage and nerve because all of this was completely against her morals and standards. (Mine too, Kate! Mine, too).

By this time, this is actually what I've come to expect and I meet her momentum and energy full on. We're passionately kissing, and clothes are flying off. Then, what I can only label as *lifeless* or *hesitation* sets in on Kate's perspective. She's still. I ask her if she is ok. The reply was that her body was shaking all over. She is not ok. I let her know it's completely fine if we stop and let's talk about this. Instead, she takes off the promise ring and launches it across the bedroom, where it rolls, clangs, and rolls some more until it lands under a door and in a closet. She has a comfortable death grip on my unit and requests that I go down on her. Absolutely! When she has finished, she calmly gets up, looks me deeply into my eyes, where I feel like my soul is being penetrated, kisses my lips and the inside of my mouth as though she was wiping the taste of herself out of me, thanks me for a "raunchy good time", and walks out with a shit-eating grin.

I learned later, that Veronica and Kate had tagged the team for this one. "Let him eat you out", she tells Kate, "And then just get up and leave and don't say anything. That will really fuck him up for a while. Who does he think he is trying to be with someone so soon anyway. After me is what I mean. Fuck!". Thanks, although I certainly did not mind. Kate was tasty, and she would always have something lingering if it worked out with her boyfriend. I hope she's happy and healthy wherever she might be. There was one thing I felt tortured by in this situation, and it was the idea that it was seemingly easy for her to remove her promise ring, get naked with me, touch me in places, and also let someone satisfy her orally. Yes, that bothered me for a bit and what came out of it, was "Real Love, Compromised." Authored 25JUL2003.

Real Love Compromised

Let's talk about life's toughest tests.

Where love is imaginary,

Feelings aren't true,

And love ends up being who is the best at sex.

Love is full of letdowns and pain.

Happiness is the key,

Relationships are few,

Love is this made-up entity that we feign.

Compromise is definitely a must.

Without it, happiness flees,

Love is entombed,

And let's not forget that element of trust.

No matter, your deeds still linger.

Even after intimacy.

I've plucked the bloom,

And yet you point the finger.

Now imagine all that you despise.

You block the memory.

Of my finger in you.

And that, my dear, is your real love compromised.

White Roses

White Roses.

Although I wish they were red.

But there will be another time.

For things like that to be said.

Let these equal the purity.

Of our new friendship.

Let them equal

Everything we've said.

Everything we've felt.

Everything we still have left to feel.

White Roses.

A symbol of a new beginning.

Never an end.

Never a petal falling off in weakness.

Not once a decaying moment.

Only endless blossoms

As far as our mortal eyes can see.

Let these white roses be for you.

A symbolic gift from me.

White Roses.

Place them in a locket.

The one you keep in your heart.

Don't underestimate the power of its charms.

Keep them wherever you keep me

And remember them when you get lonely.

Place them where your fantasies brood.

And feel no guilt, just feel… good.

Chapter 6 – Sarka (Pronounced Sharka)

I had really hurt Veronica and likewise she had hurt me. After Veronica, I made a decision to quit dating all together. 100%! I was done. I didn't want to feel hurt (tortured) any longer. I also did not want to hurt anyone, not ever again. So, I stayed sober, celibate, and hidden from the world for the duration of one entire year. It was time to "know thyself".

After grabbing my BS in Sports Medicine, I landed a position in Stockton, California as the Director of a Fitness Club for a Ford motor plant. The fitness center was a mere 600 sq ft so all we had were a few treadmills and a few dumbbells. In other words, no one ever used it which means I could remain out of sight and out of mind to all of human kind. I used the time wisely by reading as many Stephen King books as I could afford. And thinking. Lots of thinking. Lost in thoughts. Lost.

I was not devoid of human contact entirely. I had made one friend and he lived next door. I don't recall his name and as I would come to find out later, he wasn't actually a friend. Let's call him Neighbor. One night, and nearly one year after swearing off humanity, Neighbor knocks on my door and invites me to tag along to a party with him. "Sounds fun", I say and I agree to go. I'm twenty-six years old now. I've had life experiences and a long time to think about who I want to be. I consider my lot in life. I'm fully bald and I'm pulling off a nice Jason Statham look. I'm still pretty fit and by now I'm 10% body fat but I still have arm veins and abs. I seemingly have a good career but I'm broke. I'm living in California at a meager annual salary of $36k per year plus benefits. This was a time in my life when I had a nice apartment that my paycheck went to every month. It was fully furnished everywhere except the living room. For the living room, I used a camping chair with one drink holder and a moving cardboard box as my coffee table.

Every Friday, I would reward my lack of hard work with 1.5 liters of Jack Daniel's Tennessee Whiskey and cokes while watching reruns of Star Trek: The Next Generation. The next day, I would be wrecked, but it didn't really matter because I had nothing to do and nowhere to go. I would make it to the gym by 3 PM every Saturday and Sunday and for a moment of foreshadowing, I'll just indicate here Dear Reader, that I am not yet an excessive version of myself. That would not take place until I hit the ripe age of forty.

At the fitness center, I come into contact with Eccentric Lady (EL). EL is 30 years older than I am, believes in astrology, numerology, tarot reading, and has a notion about the universe and talks about it in nearly every sentence she utters. I've never heard anyone speak like this, and I'm intrigued. She provided me with a numerology and astrology profile combined. These combined profiles indicated that I'm destined for great love adventures as well as wealth beyond my imagination. The remarkable thing here, is that this version of me is actually open to it. "The universe huh?". I'm starting to feel momentum in my veins. "I'm going to be insanely successful and wealthy, hmm. And, I'm going to have great adventures in love. I start to really become introspective. I've been critically thinking about who I am, who I want to be, what I want from this life, and how I get it.

She tells me to write it down.

Write down everything you want in a woman. Write down everything you want in this life. Be bold. Go big time. And don't worry about any figure heads in your life. Be your own fucking figurehead, Michael. You're destined for it. I see your whole future ahead of you. I'm not saying it's all unicorns and leprechauns, but you don't know what you have inside of you. You have this amazing aura. You need to listen to your instincts more. You've got great ones. Listen! Listen to them and you cannot be stopped and you cannot go wrong. Oh, one more thing: your authentic self has not yet arrived. I'm sorry to tell you Michael, you have a lot of work to do and it will be fucking difficult; you'll reach the lowest of lows before your authentic self finally presents itself. Most people never reach their authentic selves. If I had to predict, I'd say right before you turn fifty, if you're still alive that is, and if you put in the effort, you will be your authentic self. I can see it. Well, shit, I already see it, so fuck that.

I'm all puzzle. My "authentic self". *If I'm still alive.* Jesus! It lingers in my thoughts like a waterfall.

I do take her advice and I write it all down and I say it out loud three times.

Dear Synchronous Universe. I just met one of your disciples. I don't know if that's the right term for it. I do plan, shortly, to look into this concept of synchronicity and the universe. Anyway, she is a nice lady. She told me that in order for me to commune with you, that I just need to write it down. What do I have to lose also, I have a lot of bandwidth I don't know what happens next because dumbshit forgot to ask a smart question. So here it goes. This is what I want. I want to find the love of my life and, become married and have kids. I want my wife to be intelligent because I think I need someone who is way smarter than I am. She and I have to be able to use our words, articulately. I want her to be faithful, moral, with a high degree of onus and accountability. I'm sorry, I don't know the rules for this so please forgive any of my mistakes and swear words. I don't like ugly chics. So, please, I want this future person to be drop dead, gorgeous. I like big boobies, and I like long, lean, tone, and tan. I like fit, slim, muscles, smells nice. She must have an exotic look to all that makes up her beauty. I want and need a woman who I would consider to be the "full package". She needs to be confident. She needs to be an Alpha-Female. I've gone through some shit, so I want her to be nice, but I also want

Page 103

someone who knows themselves. Who knows what they want to be and when and where they want to be that. I want her to want me for me and obviously I need her to want to have a lot of sex. I want her to be employed just in case something happens to me. I want her to know herself. Everything that was my biological mother and my father's wife, I want all things the opposite of those horrid assholes. Come to think of it, and not to be weird, but I'd like someone who in many regards will be like my grandmother was. Regarding my professional life. I just want to do something where I'm valued. I eventually want it to be lucrative. I want to leave behind a legacy. Please, put tools in my way and give me opportunities to learn so that I can become my authentic self. I don't really know what that means. So, if you could help me with that, then I probably will be infinitely grateful for the finite amount of time I might have on the planet. Most of all Universe, I just want balance. If I can just have a balanced life, then I will have a happy life. Also, it would be great if I could have an amazing social network and friend group. I hope I haven't asked for too much. I know that I will need to put in the effort. At twenty-seven years old now, I believe I have the discipline and wherewithal to put in the time; fucking blood (torture), sweat (ebbs), and tears (flows).

That night, I met Sarka. And yes, Dear Reader, it was love at first sight. I'm older now though. I feel that flutter, and I know that these things take time. Not everyone falls in love at first sight (don't cha ya know). I take things very slowly. I introduced myself, and I could tell she was interested. She's a Czech Republic beauty. Sexy accent, a professional tennis star, blonde, blue-eyed. Tanned. Toned. Tight. Torturously good looking. Way out of my league. And of course I'm thinking non-stop about the letter I wrote to the universe. A pervading thought is…wait, I just wrote it. Is this going to play out as some cruel fucking joke?

At some point in the night, after our introductions, she makes her way to where the Neighbor and I are catching up. The Neighbor immediately throws charm and charisma her way and she pretends like I'm the only one at the party. "Walk with me", she says plainly. And so I do. Although I've been in this scenario a few times now, I'm calm and cool. Just evaluating and being in the moment. I'm here, present, right now. I'm slightly smirking.

What's that smile about, hmm?

Nothing Sarka, I'm just happy to be here at this party and I'm glad we're having a private moment. I was looking for one, and you're pretty popular.

Do you know who I am?

No, I just met you.

Don't you follow tennis?

I do. My favorite female tennis player is Anna Kournikova.

And with that announcement came a torrential downpour of slurs and swear words in a beautiful language that I have not heard before.

I apologize. Have I insulted you?

Anna continues to be the only player that I can't get by.

I'm sorry. I'm still confused. Are you saying that you are a professional tennis player?

Dang man. Catch up. Yes, that's what I'm saying. Do you want to play a match with me?

She was being serious. And also, she had the cutest of twinkles as she said it. She was being sincere because any other man would say "no" on the spot so that his confidence would remain in tact. And then she would know right off that this was not a dude she'd consider. I thought about it for a moment just to delay our gratification.

And then with emphasis.

You're on. I'm a pretty good tennis player by the way. So, you better not be easy on me and you bring your best game. I'm being serious. I'm known to be The Upsetter. I'm like Nadal & Agassi combined. I'm being serious. What are you laughing at? Haha, you'll see.

We exchanged numbers and our date was a week later. The date was a week later but we had been on the phone every day after the party. The neighbor decided we could no longer be friends because he had invited me, and therefore, I was to forgo any dates with Sarka because they were meant to be together. Makes total sense, dude.

Listen, after the tennis match, which of course she won, she said I was actually really good and I gave her a run for her money. She felt "challenged" by me and really had to turn it up as though it were a professional match. I'm glowing. My ego is supercharged. I mean, come on Dear Reader, I was competing with a professional tennis player! In the time I spent with Sarka, which I forgot to mention is in San Franciso, we went on a lot of dates. We club. I take her sight seeing to all of the main spots in San Fran. We go so far as to start holding hands. We're the same age. She's filthy rich. I don't have any money but I'm a proud man so I pay for everything as I was taught to do by my grandma. "Always be a gentleman".

Six months of courting fly by in a flash. I realize that I'm insanely in love with this woman. This is the one. I fucking know it. There is no torture. There are no ebbs and flows. This is real and true love. She feels the same way; and I know she is not ready to admit it. Also, I have not figured out how I'm going to reconcile this huge issue where she's a superstar and I'm nobody. She does not care about that but I have become obsessed with the idea. I start to regress and start becoming SAM. I start to traverse back to "traditional". At least I'm able to recognize it though so there's hope. Is there though? I try to convince myself that the Universe is working in my corner. It's of no use. And inevitably, I fuck it all up. Here's how:

First, I wrote her a 10-page love letter. Second, I used Neighbor's computer to make her nearly 100 CDs of my favorite music. Third, I have framed and gift wrapped the one and only photo we have of each other, which is a polaroid from a San Fran Street Vendor.

Yeah. Wow. Nice gestures twenty-seven year old version of me. Your forty-seven year old self, says, "come on dumbshit, when did any of those other insanely romantic gestures work out for you?". Alas, I don't know how to travel in time, so that's just a revision.

I show up, unannounced, to her part-time San Fran residence, and to my chagrin, she's throwing a party and I can hear Neighbor in the background.

Michael, I was not expecting you. This is such a wonderful surprise. I had wondered why you did not show up to my party with your neighbor, Neighbor.

Was I invited? How?

Yes of course! I've been looking forward to seeing you. I thought you ghosted me. I haven't heard from you in a week and you haven't responded to my texts.I've missed you terribly and have been wanting to go on another date. Are you ok? *Are we ok?*

I pulled out my phone and showed her. I had not received any calls or any texts. Then it clicks. I had not had enough money to pay the bill this month. I feel embarrassed. I'm feel like a dumbass. I explain it to her. And for her it does not really compute. We've been having this 5-star luxury time and at six months she's seeing that I'm not at her level. She realizes that I might be a poor person but she has all of these feelings for me. She's wrestling.

Michael. Listen. I do not think this is the time or the place. That said, you have a lot of things in your hand. Talk to me.

Still standing in the doorway. I'm Awkward.

Sarka. I just wanted you to know, that I'm madly in love with you. We've been together for six months. I think that's a good amount of time to pass to be able to say it out loud. Look. You have to go because you're having this party. I get it. Please accept this bouquet of flowers. I think they will go nice with the party. This is a letter. Please don't read it until we have our date. This means that we should read it together on the date. And, also, I made you some CDs of my favorite songs. Music has tremendous meaning for me because of the way that I process sound. I just want to highlight a few things and it will make for a fun conversation.

And then I leaned in, kissed her on the cheek, told her again, "I love you" and drove myself home. And that was the last time I saw her in that year.

A week later and we were to meet on a date. She made the arrangements this time so I knew in my heart that she was "ok" with the news and perhaps even enjoying the CDs I made. I was sitting in a nice restaurant. I ordered a cocktail and the bread service. At this moment, the date is already five minutes past the start time. Then twenty-five. Then thirty. My phone is working again so I call her. "We're sorry, this line has been disconnected…".

Dear Reader, I spent a long time trying to find the love letter mentioned previously. I believe it was a hand written letter. Refer to Appendix 3 for the one page I was able to locate. The point is that I wrote her a tome of my feelings and professed my undying and unconditional love to her. What was I thinking? Great question. I was thinking that the written word is powerful and legacy. I was thinking that if I lay all of my cards on the table there are only two possible outcomes.1) Affirmation. 2) Oblivion. It seems like the latter was the final outcome.

Sarka completely disappeared. Sarka was an apparition now. Her social media was shutdown. Her phone was turned off. She had completely abandoned me. I was left for years wondering what in the actual fuck did I do to deserve this? I had pervasive thoughts. Was it because of my hair insomuch as I did not have any? My lack of money? Was I not athletic enough for her? Did I do something wrong? I thought I was doing everything right this time. Why is it not enough?

These questions lead into a deep dive of "knowing thyself further" and also revisiting what I want with the universe. What I can say though is that Sarka becomes the catalyst to propel me to be more than I am. I start to read more. I start to figure out that there is more and better for me in this life. I quit my corporate job and move back to Michigan. I figure out that I want to be back in the pharmaceutical industry. I land a job back in that industry in less than a few weeks time from the move. In that regard, I really start to pay attention to the details of life, my life and all of those who are in it. I start to figure out how to manage and maintain relationships. I start to understand the currency of the planet and how to manage life. I make a lot mistakes. From each, I gain tremendous wealth and I don't make the same mistakes again. I frequently engage with the universe to Revise what I want. I can feel big things happening. I can see changes in me, and so can all of my friends. I'm not so blind. I'm almost finally ready to reveal my authentic self.

Twenty years go by. I'm forty-five years old. My wife and I are in Newport Beach celebrating an anniversary. My agreement with the universe remains about *balance*. And my wife and I are not in the best of places. In fact, the relationship is still reeling due to my excessive behaviors and because SAM is in fully present. Our friends take a picture of us on the beach. And something we never do anymore, we post it to social media; both Facebook and Instagram. Suddenly my phone rings, and it's Sarka. My first thought is that my wife is about to die a tragic death. Why would Sarka suddenly be calling me? My wife has a heart condition that we've recently learned about only because I've begged her to go see a doctor after I noticed something that I cannot describe here, Dear Reader, apologies, it's too personal for her. Anyway, I believe the Universe is about to play a cruel joke on me, and keep its promise about *balance*. And so I believe that my wife will die soon because that would be the only reason to balance my life by bringing Sarka back in it.

Sarka is amused.

Mike, I just saw this beautiful photo of you and your gorgeous wife pop up.

Sarka, are you aware that we haven't spoken in twenty years? I didn't know that you had my number still and how are we connected on social media?

I know. I know. Listen. I'm in Santa Monica. Can you meet for a cup of coffee?

Fuck.

I turn to my wife, who knows about my "friend" Sarka, and explain it to her, and she says, "yeah, of course you have to go see her". And so I do.

We meet at a local Santa Monica coffee shop that is connected to a nice hotel. I notice her first and tap her on the shoulder and with a smile ear to ear, say, "Hey". She stands up and gives me the biggest of hugs. And we repeat that cycle a few times, in only the appropriate of manners of course. We both remark that we look great. It's like no time has passed at all for both of us. We're aging well. And twenty minutes has elapsed and there is the natural lull that I'm so fond of remarking on.

Sarka starts the conversation as I had hoped she would. She abandoned me after all so what could possibly be on her mind. I also don't care because I'm so happy to see her. I'm hoping the conversation, although I don't need it, will give me some kind of closure.

Michael, what was that? What were "we"?

We're both suddenly in tears. It appears that Sarka might need some closure too.

I don't know. I was hoping you could tell me. Also, thank you for that being the leading question because from my perspective, you there one day, and then suddenly you were gone. Look. I'm not trying to trudge up the past because I can tell we've both moved on. But, if you're feeling the same way I'm feeling, and it seems to me like you are, then maybe we should revisit our young selves and figure this out. Anyway, what occurs to me after a lifetime of experiences is that the best I can come up with is this. We were madly in love with each other. We didn't know if we should express it. I don't know why we would both feel that way. It's the only thing that makes sense to me. Ultimately, I think we both needed companionship. I know why I needed it. I don't know why you did.

Look at that. Mature Moderate Mike. He understands *companionship* now. He understands what Alpha-Female was trying to convey those twenty years ago.

You know Sarka, you might be my oldest friend on planet earth. Well, there's Tonya, but we're not speaking any longer. We had a massive falling out. I'm sure you remember I would often be on the phone with her.

Michael. It occurs to me that maybe you don't know about a specific detail in my life that was going on back then. Do you know?

No, I don't think so.

I'm mentioning this because you said that I *abandoned you.* I did no such thing. Oh my god. I remember that you had given me this insanely romantic letter. Who writes love letters any longer. It still stands as the most beautiful thing anyone has ever done for me. Truly.

I tried to interject that it was in fact not a love letter but she waved me away.

Michael. I left San Fran in a tizzy because my mom abruptly passed away. It was sudden and shocking and I was in no head space to deal with love matters. You didn't know this?

As a tear was welling in the side of her eye before it made its way to the duct where gravity took over.

I'm sorry for the loss of your mom, Sarka. That is a new detail for me. Truly, I had not known this before. Suddenly, twenty years ago makes so much sense to me. Thank you for that.

We had been leaning in towards each other and the conversation was rapid. At the realization of the loss of her mother as well as the loss of each other, and the reason why, suddenly everything made sense. I sat back in my chair. Sarka did too. We sat in silence for a very long time. I think we were, the both of us, going backwards in time to piece it all together and also to process *what is* versus *what could have been.*

The rest of the conversation, which was six total hours (felt like 6 minutes) was us catching up as one might expect of an old friend. Pictures of our life. Her child. My Frenchies, etc. And then, when it was time to depart, there was this lingering tension between us. You see, as companions, we had not explored each other physically. There was no time, and now I knew, no room for that exploration. We had held hands, we had embraced, we had kissed like Europeans do, but never once were we in the throes of passion. I'm fairly certain that each of us had concluded this might be the last time we would ever see each other. And to be fair, this is another synchronous fucking moment that probably shouldn't be occurring at all. So, we embrace it one more time. And for the first time in two decades of knowing each other and actually feeling something for someone once upon a time, we kiss passionately. We both let it happen. And there is no regret here. And this might just be a big fucking Revision but I step backwards because I realize the love and life I have with my wife. When I step back, Sarka steps forward for more. She is also married, but she has announced to me in the conversation that she is fucking miserable and it's a marriage of convenience for their child. They step out on each other when there is an occasion to do so. An occasion just like this. I embrace her one more time. I walk away. I do turn back. I do smile.

The fucking torture of love.

<u>Gliding to Your Light</u>

In my dreams
I'm floating by
Gliding through the light.

Suddenly
I see you there
In your blinding shine.

I see tears
Upon your cheek
And also your smile.

Hand in hand
We walk away
Walking miles and miles.

Lost in thought
We glide away
Hoping not to wake.

In our love

We climb inside
At least for a day.

This is where
I go and hide
When things aren't all right.

In my dreams
I'm floating by
Gliding to your light.

Chapter 7 – Aikaterini (AKA, Aikaterini the Freak)

While living in North Carolina, as a Lab Tech for a Contract Manufacturing Organization, I would pursue odd jobs to help with the rent, bills, and student loans. One of those odd jobs was actually to put my BS degree to good use. I became certified as a personal trainer with the World Instructor Training School (WITS). And three times a year, I would train a small class of students on how to be a Personal Trainer. I did this for the money; $25 an hour was good money for me back then. And to be honest with you Dear Reader, I actually did this to meet beautiful, like minded and fit women. It's no Revision to tell you that once each six-week class had concluded, that I had a beautiful woman to date after. There were several one and done(s) as I like to say yet one stood with me, off and on, for a period of three years. Her name is Aikaterini and she liked to be called, "Aikaterini the Freak" or "Freakie".

For an apt description, please refer to Saturday Night Live's Mary Katherine Gallagher's Superstar character. Aikaterini the Freak and Molly Shannon are twins (in appearance). She wasn't a bombshell but she had layers that sparked an immediate attraction. She had a type, and it was me. This version of me was a lost puppy that needed saving. It's probably one year after Sarka and I really don't know who I am anymore, even though I've told the Universe exactly who I want to be. She lives in Charlotte. She's a starving artist. Her medium is the camera. She's quite gifted at it but does not know how to market herself. She and I are on the same level financially speaking. We're broke. And we don't care about that as we begin to court one another. Dear Reader, I'm still living the same pattern of my life in this version of myself. I'm still all love at first sight and shit, except this time it truly is different. It was not love at first sight and instead, it was love at first kiss, which occurred on our first date.

I was living in Lenoir, North Carolina and she agreed to meet in Lenoir, again, traveling from Charlotte which is a good 90 minute commute. Thinking about Veronica, I thought maybe this was a ruse for Aikaterini to spend the night after our date. I wasn't going to say "no". I would end up offering this at the end of the night when I receive the sudden and pleasurable kiss good night. When I offered, she looked me up and down, and considered it. Then she said, "Michael, I totally want to fuck you right now. You don't know me though. I'm all kinds of crazy; you'll see. Get to know me a little. In a few weeks if you still want to get it on, then I'm down". I stood there feeling high and dry as she drove her Ford Tauras back to Charlotte. I didn't sleep that night as you might expect. I needed electricity for a ground.

Being with Aikaterini is 100% torment for my soul. The output of that torment is nearly 100 poems. Since you're still with me,

Dear Reader, you know that that is the epitome of torment. In two weeks, both of us are already professing our undying love for each other. The sex is the best I've ever had and she's quite gifted in all aspects of intercourse. Shows me things that I had not yet even heard of before. One time, she offered me this tantalizing fantasy.

Michael. My biggest fantasy regarding you. I want to pick a beautiful Asian woman for you. I want to watch you fuck her. What I mean is, I want my face to be near the collision of the uglies. And when you're ready, I want you to pull out of her and come all over of my face. God it makes me so fucking horny.

This admission of this fantasy would always result in the actual act except for the Asian woman part. If you're wondering, I always declined the offer to fulfill this fantasy. I was thinking that Aikaterini was definitely marriage material and well, that fantasy, was just not something I could oblige her on morally speaking. I would view it as cheating on her and would not be able to get over it. Plus, I thought it would be a trap at some point to laud it over my head as some kind of break-up exit strategy. At forty-seven, if single, I would now say yes. I view sex as just sex and if my wife gave me an opportunity, I'd take it. I'd still be able to be in love with her; it would not be about how insufficient she is, as she would say if I were to cheat on her. I would never. I have never. However, as I've come to learn in my late forties, I can love many women if it were an option. I do love many women but there is only one woman who I love in that marital way, and to be ultra clear here, it's my current wife. (Which one, Mike? This is a Revision).

As an artist, Aikaterini takes me on a journey to my own self-discoveries. I have body image issues. So the first thing she suggests, is, *why don't we shave all this hair off. I believe there is a beautiful body under there.* So, we get in the shower together, and in a very sensual way, Aikaterini lathers my whole body with shaving cream, including my scalp. We're both in a steamy shower, naked, and I'm raging hard, which she caters too every so often, with an *accidental* bump, a brush, or a grip.

After the shaving is completed, we both stand naked together in lengthy mirror. And there I am, arm veins, abs, chiseled. Statue of David in appearance. Also, we discover that my head is perfectly round. It's a beautiful, bald head. I no longer have image issues. And I strut around like King Shit. She notices and it's a huge turn on for her and now we're making love every single day, sometimes two times a day. I can't keep my hands off of her. She walks around in boy-shorts and I walk around banging into things with my boner.

Then, Aikaterini has another brilliant idea. Let's do a photo shoot. Let's just see where it takes us. We end up winning Seattle, Erotic Photo contest. We angled the camera so that we would appear entirely androgenous. *Who is the male? Who is the female?* No one could tell and it became the talk of the whole show. To be clear, we won first place for our entry entitled, "Androgyny".

By the way, Dear Reader, Aikaterini ends up being the one who teaches me the concept of synchronicity. After all, it was her goofy and clumsy self that accidentally launched the book on synchronicity at my head in the bookstore.

Aikaterini is the first individual that I live with. We can debate that Melisa and I lived together too but it's not totally accurate, considering that we each still had our own place. Aikaterini has moved into my two bedroom apartment because she can no longer afford her place and is trying to survive as an artist in downtown Charlotte. We've been dating one month. What could go wrong?

I learn that Aikaterini is a recovering sex, alcohol, and drug addict. That's okay. After one year of being together and living together, she asks me if I can please remove all of the alcohol out of the place because she's having difficulty with seeing me have an occasional drink. I oblige. If I need a drink, I'll just go out with one of the dudes. No problem.

Aikaterini is not working. I'm working full time 8-10 hours a day. Aikaterini grows listless. I can see a dark cloud forming and it follows her around. I'm growing more and more concerned about her mental wellness on the daily basis. We're suddenly in screaming matches. We break up. We get back together. It's a cycle that repeats every few weeks and I feel myself growing mad. I'm writing her poetry and letters every day, multiple times a day. Also, we're madly in love with each other. We're loyalists. Neither one of us is going to go away completely. We're addicted to each other. In a home that already has one addict, it is not safe for anyone when now there are two.

Then, one tawdry day, I arrive home from work and see that all of her things are packed up. Without any discussion at all, she sits me down and provides wretched news.

Michael. I'm sorry. I'm sorry that I'm going to hurt you. I don't want to. I need to find myself. I need to figure out who I am and who I want to be. And there is nothing here (except you) for me any longer. I'm moving to Seattle, Washington. I'm going to take this awesome education you gave me and I'm going to start some kind of personal training studio there. I think my chances of success are much better there than here. So, I don't know if this is goodbye forever, or so long temporarily.

I was grimace and tearing. I decide that I'm going to stay silent and just see what happens next.

Aren't you going to say something, Michael?

What would you like for me to say I know you by now. You've already made this decision. One where I'm not included as per the usual order of events. Everything has been shit for a while now and you know I'm not going to break up with you, so this makes perfect sense to me. Thank you, actually, for relieving me of that burden. Listen. I fucking love you. I'm available to catch up with you if you want to. If you want space, take all of the fucking space you need.

Aren't you going to vie for me? Like, even a little. Come on.

Aren't you going to ask me to come with you? That's what I thought. Safe travels and take care.

And then I watched her get into her car. The flood gaits were completely open at this time. We lived in a small apartment complex where everyone knew everyone and also what was going on. We had attracted a live-studio audience for this event. She did not hit the brakes. She did not wave goodbye. And just like that, she was gone. One of my neighbors approached me and he said the following.

I'm so sorry man. Tough loss. I thought you'd like to know that she let me fuck her once while you were out of town at some wedding or some shit. She's a good fucking lay man!

And then I laid him out. And now you know Dear Reader, three of the four where I'm 4-0.

I'd like to offer a love poem from this period. I'll admit to you Dear Reader, that I had planned on letting you glimpse all of the poetry from this period. It's too much. You'll give me feedback on that end and I can tell you in advance that this volume has a sequel. Perhaps, the sequel will provide sate on this subject.

Collisions – Authored 22NOV2003

And so you've inspired.

Another insane moment.

Where some lost soul

Gets to express his torment.

Understand that this is good.
At least in our case.
However, I'm left to wonder.
What you perceive during your day.

Do you stop to stare
At life's exacting precisions?
Or instead, do you notice
All of the random collisions?

In all aspects except one
I'm aware of the first.
And my awareness of the second
Causes my heart to burst.

And I'm not judging,
But in all fairness,
You are the cause
Of this sudden awareness.

And I what I coin 'us'
Is a multitude of collisions,
Where the randomness, it seems,

Is destined to rule this dominion.

I remember our first collision.
A melding of the minds.
Where we easily accepted
What was about to collide?

The thoughts flowed freely.
With mutual fruition.
So ,we eagerly anticipated
The physical collisions.

And those that followed
Have left us in bliss.
The vibrating words.
The impact of a kiss.
The way our hands
Have a mind of their own.
Rummaging through skin.
Exploring lines of unknown.

An insatiable appetite
With an acceptance of trust.
A mind-blowing reciprocate
Of emotional lust.

And thus far
We've barely scratched the surface.
And I'm left to believe
That this is way too perfect.

But those thoughts of doubt
Are pummeled to pieces.
And my fervor for you
Continually increases.

And when I think about us,
I rely on intuition.
And to know that already
Allows me to savor these collisions.

Like when we are close
And the darkness is all around,
The thumping of our hearts
Becomes this distinguished sound.

Or when our bodies
Are slamming at the hips,
Producing enough passion
To sink battleships.

The tingling ecstasy
From that wonderful friction,
If I had to predict,
You'll be my greatest addiction.

And whenever I see you
These collisions take place.
The randomness of it all
You've allowed me to embrace.
And so now that I see
What makes up the random,
We can enjoy them together,
We can enjoy them in tandem.

And I know that there's feelings
That we're keeping inside.
And to be honest,
I look forward for those to collide.

When that happens
It will be the greatest collision,
Producing a force so great
We'll be thrown into submission.

Our minds, bodies, and souls

Will have to surrender.

But we'll be left

With our greatest adventure.

Until that moment

We'll randomly collide,

And when appropriate,

Unleash what's inside.

Three months elapse. There are big changes for me. I decided that the ghost of Aikaterini is too much for me to process. I see her everywhere I go and the apartment is a glossary of memories, great, bad, and indifferent. I land a job in Lansing, Michigan. It's the start of a new life for me. In those three months, I had processed the breakup relatively unscathed, and I had the mindset that "everything is going to be okay". I'm registered for a Master of Science degree at Michigan State University and classes will begin in the fall, the same as my new full time job. My dad even agrees to help me move from North Carolina and for the first time in a long time, everything is perfect.

Literally, the morning that we arrive to my new East Lansing Apartment, Aikaterini gives me a call. She was just checking on me to see how I was doing. It's really nice to hear her voice. On the other hand, I thought I was over her by now and I realize I'm being sucked back in very quickly. I say, "Listen Aikaterini, we've been apart for three months now. I certainly have missed, and at the same I was thinking that I was over you. I'm not. So, with that, I'd really appreciate if we can end the call. I hope everything is okay with you and that you're finding yourself out there. I fucking love you. I have to go". I hang up the phone without allowing her to say anything more. She called me back, and I answered it.

Michael. What the fuck. Can we please talk for a few minutes?

No. I'd be happy to listen, though.

Thank you. You know me. I can talk talk talk. So, I just want to reciprocate. I fucking love you still and I've missed you terribly. I can't get you out of my head. I hate the way that we ended things. I need to know where are you right now?

That's a strange question. Funny that you started there. Okay, well, I'm in Michigan. I've landed a really good job and I'll be starting school up again soon too for a higher education. I had the offer letter in my hand the last time I saw you.

Why didn't you tell me about this? Depending on things, I might have come with you.

Why didn't you ask me to go with you? Then, it would have been totally natural for me to give this exciting update. Depending on things huh? As in, ensuring you'd have all that you need in order for you to discover yourself, correct Well, East Lansing could offer you an opportunity to fulfill that dream you mentioned and I could have totally helped you set it all up.

Listen Michael! I need to see you.

To be honest, I'm not sure that's a good idea. Remember what we used to fight about. None of that shit has changed. But, if you must, then, and I didn't know this when I got the job so it's another synchronous moment, I will have quality oversight over a contracted filling operation that I will be traveling for once a quarter and it's in Spokane, Washington which is only a short flight for me to see you in Seattle. It's a short drive too and I believe this is a sign from the Universe to be together still. What do you think?

Fuck yeah it is! Superstar!

When she picks me up from the airport, it's apologetic and there are sobs from both parties. We run into an airport bathroom and immediately have sex. We both cry at the end because not only have our souls missed each other but so have our bodies and the body never lies. After, Aikaterini announces to me that in addition to her personal training gig, she's now a go-go dancer in a nightclub and is also studying to become a Yoga Master. I'm still Mr. Morality, and I confuse go-go dancing with stripping so we get into a huge fight and break up. But we get back together every time I'm coming into town. And it inspires a shit ton of poetry. Here's one where I know love is starting to develop into hate. They're not really that different.

Definitions – Authored 28DEC2004, Revised 11SEP2024

You:

One thousand shades of gray.

I believe in this right now

But it will change by the end of the day.

I am defined by my past.

Structured by misery and loss.

I believe that change is what lasts.

I am atypical and challenge normalcy.

I can't help but be in a constant fight with myself.

I will go through life and never claim dependency.

In the end I know that everyone leaves.

Simultaneous striving for loneliness and perfection.

I am a success in the fact that I still breathe.

Take away the fantasy and I am destroyed.

I cease to function.

It's the fantasies that keep me employed.

The fantasies will help me realize my dreams.

Family and boyfriends have kept those at bay.

And rid of all of that I'll prove it, you'll see.

I'll have what I want and be able to be free.

I am my own best friend.

Reality is my enemy.

I ignore my own clock and can't seem to decide.

The older I get the harder it becomes.

And I know that time is not on my side.

I will not be burdened by other's needs.

I can only pretend to know what it is I want.

Selfishness, in all of my lives, is my only creed.

I must reshape myself every other year.

If you knew me then, you would not recognize me now.

And if you see me again, I promise, you should stay clear.

Me:

Nothing but the black and the white.

Mostly blinded by structure.

Don't bother me with issues, I like it light.

A prisoner of my childhood.

I must impress, I must be the best.

If I haven't accomplished something, then I am no good.

Searching for the American Dream
With the wife, the family, the house, and the car.
Only because everyone else has those things.

And that is where I'll find happiness.
Along with my hobbies and my routine.
I always want more I must confess.

I can survive in the fantasy.
Even tolerate it for a while.
But I always come back to the reality.

Reality pushes me through my own miseries.
I can control the bottle.
My sobriety is controlled and expressed through my poetry.

I'm helpless and hopeless and romantic.
Always in search of the one.
This keeps me protected, anxious, and frantic.

I base myself and strive on what could be.
I am defined by the future.
The past stays where it is…behind me.

I am aware of and understand my character flaws.

I do try and keep them under wraps.

It's one of my mysteries I have yet to solve.

I try to be everything to everyone while remaining true.

I become angered when I don't maintain that status.

One day I'll understand exactly what I am supposed to do.

Us:

An enchanting potion.

Roller coaster rides.

Explosions of emotion.

Not meant for this time.

Dear Reader, for the first time in this Volume, I want to offer the perspective of my counterpart. Below is a letter from Aikaterini herself. And that's all I can stomach any further on this subject. I probably did not do well in this chapter, and well, it's because I have genuinely put Aikaterini behind me and I have over 100 poems to prove it. Writing this was difficult because, like a Terminator, I deleted the Aikaterini files after Terminating her from my existence.

She broke up with me, but you get me. T is for Terminator.

michael,

it's sad that things have to end this way but we need to remember to be honest with each other and ourselves. so on that note, we both know that dragging this out any longer would be extremely painful. that is what i was trying to tell you this weekend and i couldn't believe you actually wanted to still see me. I am so sorry for hurting you. i was being selfish and i feel horrible for it. I think we both were being selfish. we both had moved and were starting our lives over and we wanted someone to be there for us during the transition.

change is scary and as much as i may thrive on it and traveling the world, it still sucks being w/o you. we both realized last week that we have different values and different goals. we've known this for a while but i think we finally decided to see things for what they really are and quit holding onto the fantasy.

i love you so much michael and am eternally grateful for everything you have done for me. i have never shared so much with someone and will never forget the love between us. i'm not right for you either and me thinking about marriage and kids was a way for me to think about how i would fit into your life b/c I wanted this so bad. i'm sorry for telling you these things and getting your hopes up. i guess i was willing to do anything to try and make things work. call it deseperation but i call it love. and how much we love each other shows even now b/c we are finally letting each other go. as painful as it is and will be for a while, it is the right thing to do.

as far as the pictures go, if you want to send me money then i can get them to you faster. i will send your shirt and book this week. and of course i want the poetry. it will remind me of the love we shared and yes that will be painful but you can't have the sweet w/o the sour. i can never express to you how much you mean to me and how having you in my life has changed me for the better. Of course we need time to get over each other but maybe in the future we

can stay in touch. it's hard to imagine you not being in my life. i will miss you terribly and feel so lost w/o you for a long time. we both have a lot of things to work on.

i know you will be happy b/c you are so passionate about everything you do. you treated me like a goddess and any women would be extremely lucky to spend a lifetime with you. i just wish that could have been me.

you are the greatest love of my life too Michael Antonio Delitala. it's so hard to say goodbye so i will just say, see you next lifetime my love.

i love you madly, the only way i know how

Aikaterini

Agreement

I've mentioned this in previous laments.

Our nature has inspired another insane moment.

Welcome to a chapter where true love is also a state of torment

One thing we have, at the very least, is the acknowledgment.

And in that, our feelings continue to ferment.

For you, our love, and the rest of the world, let this serve as a testament.

These words, by pen or mouth, are stronger than the strongest cement.

No water, fire, or earthly disaster could make a mark or a dent.

No person will stand in the way; our will must not be broken or bent.

We must brave through the distance, time, and the elements.

With all of the disclaimers I could possibly conceive, here now is our agreement:

We do not know what the future holds next.

We can not find that in some story or some text.

We understand it will be difficult and complex.

We realize now that this might be the greatest test.

We will have to persevere through a plethora of stress.

We are not kidding and we dare not jest.

Understanding fully that it may not be for the best.

But for now and in the months that progress:

No one else are we allowed to caress.

No kissing, touching, fondling or nakedness.

And only with each other are we allowed to have sex.

Chapter 8 – Tonya's Outback Steakhouse Story

After I completed Chapter 2, Dear Reader, I felt a sense of anguish and dread. How could I possibly have left things that way with Tonya for what is now twenty years ago. I went through my phone, which is two decades of new phones and I know you know what I mean given the way that technology has advanced. Tonya is not in my contacts. I scroll through my social media contacts and followers. I see that I am following Tonya on what appears to be three handles of hers. I reached out to her on two of them.

First message.

"Hey Tonya – I was wondering if you'd be open to a quick chat."

Gave her my number.

"Text first and then I can call you. Mike".

Second message.

"Hey Tonya. I was wondering if you would be open to a conversation. Text me first if you are open to this and then I can call you. Mike".

With a postscript of my phone number.

To my immediate surprise she immediately texted me. "Hey Mike! It's T!".

I call her and the first words out of her mouth are, "You're calling me to tell me about your book".

What the fuck! How do you know that?

We used to talk about it all the time.

We did? Listen, we can talk about that because that's actually going to be a real thing soon.

Stuttering. Bumbling.

Listen, Tonya, I'm writing Volume 2.

I read her the introductory paragraph. She's blown away by it.

You are chapter 2. I just now wrote it and in so doing, I relived the egregious act where I was violent towards you. I mean. Um. Did I ever apologize to you for that?

Mike, no, but we moved way past that a long time ago.

I'm confused. What does it mean "that we moved past that a long time ago". And instead of staying in that moment we move on and catch up just like no time has gone by at all. Danielle (my wife) and I have been having a lot of conversations lately about what real friendship looks like. And not to be on a tangent, but this conversation that Tonya and I are having is what real friendship looks like. You hop on the phone after a decade and a half of silence and instantly move and groove "like old times". I read to her the whole first and second chapter.

Listen Mikey Your portrayal is accurate. But you're forgetting a very important detail. We were drunk as fuck, you did take it too far, and it ended the night early, but I was in to you. I had my hands all over you. I was dancing with you. I wore tight spandex pants so that I could feel 'you' when I was grinding on you. I remember, we were close to thirty by now and I was still unsure of my feelings for you. I forgave you immediately because of our unconditional love for each other. Wait. I'm thinking. I'm trying to in my mind to piece together the timeline a little bit. Give me a minute. Got it! Don't you remember meeting with me at Outback Steakhouse?

I had no idea what she was referring to and asked for a little context.

You had asked me to meet you, as a date, at Outback Steakhouse. You don't remember this?

I didn't and said as much.

I remember it being weird for me. Like, you didn't smile when you saw me. You didn't stand up to hug me. I thought maybe I was going to get an apology. Instead, it was like you were on a mission. It was like you had an agenda. And then you spoke to me. Seriously, you don't remember any of this.

Tonya, I really don't. My therapist says there are two versions of Mike. There are more than two but for the sake and sanity of our conversation. I believe you. What you're saying sounds like me. This would be known as Terminator Mike. Where I have an objective, I have an agenda, and nothing and no one stops me from completing the mission. We'll talk about the other version later. I need you to please help me, if you're still willing, to tell me what happened. Because as I've learned about Terminator Mike, he is able to delete files. This sounds like something I would have deleted.

Are you fucking kidding me?

I wish I was. I'm terribly sorry. It is totally up to you and I won't press.

Tonya and I are both crying in this moment. I think for both of us in this moment in particular, things that were left unresolved are now starting to make some sense. There is also a realization breeding between us but neither of us are ready to admit it yet.

Ok then. We're going to do this. You said, "Tonya, you know I love you and that the love I share for you now is that of a good friend. I'm getting married soon. I can no longer be your friend in the way that we are friends right now. You're warmth for me, and affection for me, and sometimes your possessiveness of me can no longer be a part of my life. I've met my soulmate and the natural order of becoming married disallows this because it is discourteous and disrespectful to the relationship. I know you. And there was something that you recently did, which is just a 'Tonya' thing, but it has provoked a very rigorous argument between myself and my betrothed. It may have nearly ended things. And although I will miss you, that simply cannot be.

What Tonya reminded me of was that she had sent some kind of text with a phrase such as "My Mikey…" which was just what Tonya does and who she is. She shared with me in this moment that it is something that has actually plagued her and her relationships.

Then, you just got up from the table and were trying to leave. I begged you to stay. I literally got on my hands and knees and begged you to please stay so that we could talk it out. You were crying. I was crying. You could only mutter, "I'm sorry", and walked out. For a very long time, this would serve as one of the most defining and devastating chapters of my life. To have been friends for so long, to have actually loved each other for so long, and in an instant, one where you're still alive and on the planet, not have any more contact with you, not get a chance to see you become married, well, yeah, that fucking hurt for a really long fucking time.

And then she lightly chuckled.

What are you going to do, Mike? You know. We were so young. I had my chance with you and I didn't take it. Life would probably be so much different. The "Phoenix Thing" would not have happened for one thing. You know about that right?

And Dear Reader, I will admit that both Tonya and I can't recall where in our timeline the "Phoenix Thing" occurred and that is Tonya's tragic story and it is not meant for you unless she deems it so in her own works someday. Please accept our collective apology on that subject. It is relevant though.

Tonya, it's not lost to me that we're getting along right now famously as old friends would. Sunny and I have a huge social network out here in California and the majority of them are women. I, often, go to concerts and musical festivals with these women and Sunny does not attend these events. It's a running joke between us actually that there is second wife and on occasion, but only when she admits it, third wife. I feel fairly confident that she'd be ok with us being friends again. You know, within the normal confines and boundaries of platonic love.

Tonya accepted those terms immediately and we are good friends again.

T is for Tonya. T is for Tight, Toned, and Tanned. T is for fucking Torture. And for Tonya, she would remain tortured throughout the remainder of her days. I got to see her one more time. I was at a Festival for books in Chicago and asked her to travel from Michigan to see me. She obliged. We met in my hotel lobby and made our way to the bar. We had a very good conversation Dear Reader, like old friends who have not skipped a beat. During this conversation, Tonya reveals to me that she has stage 4 lymphoma. She looks great on the outside, but her insides are liquefying. She tells me that she agreed to meet me in person because she only has one month to live and well, "I don't give a fuck about anything anymore, Mikey. Might as well have one more moment of happiness for whatever the fuck that is worth. This moment means so much to me, you have no idea. I fucking love you. You have always been the one and I thought I'd have more time. You know? Life changes, people die, I was holding out for you if your life changed. Like a divorce. Or a death, not that I would impart that on anyone.". When the conversation reached its natural conclusion, Tonya, stood up, we held each other forever. She kissed me fully on the lips like Europeans do. She walked away. She did not glance back. She did not wave goodbye. There was no sign of smirk or smile. There was a dark cloud that seemed to shroud her and follow her.

One month later to the very day, her mom called me and told me the inevitable news. We had a good cry together and we reminisced about the good old days.

This was a story about love. Rather, the ebbs and flow of love. Actually, the fucking torture of it.

The End

Epilogue...

The Editor will no doubt ask me what this Volume is about. This Volume is about our blindspots. Dear Reader, I would encourage you to pick up <u>Thanks for the Feedback</u> by Douglas Stone & Sheila Heen. I believe that if every individual on the planet decided to read that book, then we might all actually have world peace. I'm not kidding. Getting to your authentic self, including visiting and revising until corrected, all of your blindspots and you will be rid of any angst you have in the past, present, and future.

This book is about the noticeable patterns of our everyday lives. We are creatures of habit. And we don't have to be. How many times did I write the phrase, "and it was love at first sight". "Too numerous to count" as we like to say in Quality Control microbiological testing. This book is a self-realization journey to ensure that the noticeable patterns of my past, remain there – in the past!

Stubborn Asshole Mike (SAM) is still alive by the way. My wife and I joke about him a lot, especially when he resurfaces. Whoa, hey Sam, shut the fuck up and go hence to which you came! In a way then, this Volume is about not just recognizing the pattern, but also keeping it at bay. Why? So that you can be your authentic self. Your authentic self is a super hero waiting to burst through your everyday garb. I'm not kidding. When I finally arrived (very recently) to this version of Michael A. Delitala, The Revisionist, I have become my authentic self. Good things happen to your authentic self. Good things can happen when you're not being authentic. But mostly only bad things continue to happen when you are inauthentic.

All of this happened exactly as it had to happen. How else can one become emotionally mature? I challenge you, Dear Reader, to not only decide for yourself what was real and what was fiction, but to find your authentic self. I would love if when you found them you messaged me on my website which you can find on the back cover of this book.

All of this happened so that I could be the person right for my person. She loves that the past has shaped me into the creature I exist as today. As The Revisionist which has become an alter ego of mine. We have tantalizing conversations. They will make their way to you in future volumes.

Finally, this volume is about Synchronicity.

Dear Reader, Thank you for taking this on.

Until next time.

Afterword...

Gavino and his wife Malgeun are hand in hand walking effortlessly through the streets of New York.

Gavino turns to Malgeun and says, "Hey Baby. Did you hear that?"

"Hear what", she quizzes back.

"Okay, never mind…"

Appendix 1 – Letter to Veronica – 05FEB2001

Dearest Veronica,

Oh, I don't even know how to write this to you but I want to give you something that most people don't get when unfortunate things like this happen. I want to give you closure in all of this. I've found that sometimes I still think about past relationships because I never got closure on any of them. Well, I want you to have closure to make this as painless as possible so that you can move on in a quick manner.

Would you like to know what all of this has really been about? It's been about timing Veronica. The timing for us is our enemy. I have no doubt in my mind that if we had found each other two years from now, we'd have fallen in love just as easy and would've been perfect for each other. But, you have been held down all of your life. Your parents have sheltered you, other boyfriends (probably myself included) have sheltered you and right now you are at a point in your life where you are breaking away from all of that sheltering. And I can't be responsible for just being somebody else that has held you back. You are at the time when you need to go out and be yourself without a care in the world, where you don't have to think about anybody else caring for you and getting mad at you for not being courteous. You have to go out and break some hearts, have heart to hearts with your friends about things that are bothering you, drink, get wasted, party all night long, and have adventures. And you have to believe me Veronica, everybody goes through that part of life wishing they hadn't done certain things, but that's a part of growing up. We all have to do them, and once we get it out of us, we don't do them anymore, but we're glad we had the experience of them to make us better people, mature people, ready to handle what life throws at us people. And I only know this because that's how it was for me and it's how its been for anyone I've ever had a conversation with. And I'm so sorry Veronica, but until you've gotten all of that out of you, there just isn't room for us. I can't watch you go through that, I've sat back and watched for eight months now, and with each new step you take, I get more and more hurt and more miserable. I've tried to not care, but I can't help it, I care too much. Except that my care turns into rage because of circumstances that I just don't understand. And then I get absolutely insane and instead of trying to understand, that this is what you need to do, I fight with you. We just can't do that anymore, it's so unhealthy.

And maybe for me it's about attention. I'll admit, when you started working at Target, and made new friends, a lot of attention I got from you suddenly disappeared. It still is missing. At the very beginning of our relationship, we were so into each other. Now, half the time, we don't even know what's going on in each other's life. It just doesn't work that way for people who are serious about each other. And I can't pretend any longer that it does. I need you in my *life* Veronica not just a day here or a week at the end of the year. I need you now, in the present, everyday. And that's another problem, we can't do that yet, but I can't wait any longer. I'm almost 24 and you are 19, there's so much I want to do with you but I can't. It's a serious issue with me. And by no means is that your fault, it's just the way life is right now. Basically, I need more of you! But I can't have more of you and it's killing me. Like I said, you have to go out and learn to be you first before you can be serious with anybody else. And for me, I'm looking for serious, I'm looking for my life partner, but you can't be that now, there's too much you have to get out of you first.

I know that you think that a lot of this is probably bullshit. But take some time with it. I'm not going anywhere for at least three more years Veronica. I've got one full year of Eastern left, and then I'll probably take a year off of school, then I've got two full years of another degree to get. Not to mention that right now, even as I'm typing this, I have people who want to offer me Corporate Fitness positions with their company, here in Michigan. So, I'm not going anywhere for a while. What I'm trying to say is, that if we give it some time apart, where you can do the things you need to do, and me too, then who knows Veronica? Who knows? So I say give it some time right? Think about it for a moment. All of your life you have been held down.mYou've gone from one relationship directly into another relationship. You've never been able to figure yourself out, or had time to do things that you love. You haven't been able to develop a love for yourself. And I know this sounds bad, but if we stay together now, and struggle through this, and then eventually get married, later on, you will divorce me. You will resent me for trying to stop you from going through the motions of your life in regards to the fun you need to have. You'll want to suddenly go through those motions later on, and we'll just get divorced. I know you hate it when I say this but I've seen it happen too many times. People get serious about each other when they're too young, and things fall apart later. It's better to do all of this now.

There are other issues Veronica. You know I'm a realist. And when I think about our future right now, I don't see a good one. I don't like your friends. I see them influence you in ways that disgust me. It's an issue for me. But I made a serious mistake when I asked you to change all of that. I'm sorry for that. You have to be the one to pick your friends and the activities you partake in. Your friends are the ones who are going to be there for you as you do all of those things that need to be done. I apologize for trying to change you. Your dad is an issue for me as well. I know he's trying to do what's best for you, but he shouldn't hold you back from me just because I'm older than you. Not to mention, the racism. The other night when I had dinner at your house, I just couldn't take anymore how both you and he were talking about people. That's not your fault either. You've been raised to think like that. It disgusted me to hear about how when you were three or four, that you were using words like 'nigeroo'. What I'm saying is, I don't want my own children raised in that manner. I don't want them growing up thinking that the majority of black people are 'ignorant, and lazy'. I don't judge people until I see what they are about. Our happiness is an issue for me. And we are not happy. We are in love yes, but we are not happy. But I take the blame for that. I can't be happy with us right now because I've done all of the things that you still need to do and I know what all of that is about. You have to do those things Veronica, but you have to be single to do them. So, it's a catch 22.

You know, on paper I make this sound so easy. But you have got to believe me that this is the hardest thing I've ever done. Last night, I wanted to keep you because your tears overwhelmed me so much. I am so much in love with you, and to see those tears, and to know that I'm causing them hurt me so bad. We both have a lot of hurt that has been caused by each other. I think that it's too much to reconcile right now. If we really want this to work, then we need to go away from each other for awhile. I know, it's not what I want either, but we have to be happy about us. All I can say to comfort both of us, is that maybe later on in life we can truly start again. All day long today, my heart was heavy; it was like I was drowning on my own breath. It's because the realization of losing the love of my life was too real. I made it real last night, but then it was okay again, and then today, it wasn't. I know I'm not making sense right now but this is all so complicated.

I also want you to know, that I've cherished all we've done together. I always have that; nobody will ever be able to take that away. You are locked away in my heart, and I will always have a special place there just for you. I'll never ever forget about you. I will love you forever until the day I die Veronica. It truly has been a pleasure to love you and I have absolutely no regrets about our relationship. I will miss your smile so much. I will miss your chocolate eyes and your long, curly hair. I will miss your spontaneity, and your confidence. I will miss all of you!

Please understand my reasons Gorgeous. Try to just move on quickly. I've said this before, but I want it here too. You are smart, you have an awesome personality, and you are so beautiful. I promise you Veronica, someone will you make you happy again sooner than you think. I wish it was me, but we have to be apart for a while. If it's meant to be Veronica, we will get back together, but don't hold yourself back waiting. That's not fair, go out and live life, it's what I want you to do. Show the world who you are.

Well, I'm not sure myself, but I think I've got it all out. I am so hoping, or counting on something though. If it's not too difficult, for either of us, I'm hoping that we'll at least stay in touch. Maybe we can be each other's stepping-stone until we're ready to try it again. We started off as great friends with some sort of connection;

I want to go back to that. I want us to be friends, and keep in touch. In my mind, it's the best thing to do, and if we can go there, to me, it means, later on we can try it again. Just be my friend for a while Veronica. Friends love each other too you know. I'm not saying it will be easy, but we can help each other through this. And don't think I'm abandoning you either, because I'm not, you've got to do what you've got to do right now. Unfortunately, that doesn't work for me. I'm so sorry for all of the pain I've caused you.

I'll always love you Veronica my seductress!

Love always,
Michael.

Appendix 2 – Nine Inch Nails, The Fragile

She shines

In a world full of ugliness

She matters

When everything is meaningless

Fragile

She doesn't see her beauty

She tries to get away

Sometimes

It's just that nothing seems worth saving

I can't watch her slip away

I won't let you fall apart

I won't let you fall apart

I won't let you fall apart

I won't let you fall apart

She reads the minds of all the people as they pass her by

Hoping someone will see

If I could fix myself I'd

But it's too late for me

I won't let you fall apart

I won't let you fall apart

I won't let you fall apart

I won't let you fall apart

We'll find the perfect place to go where we can run and hide

I'll build a wall and we can keep them on the other side

But they keep waiting

And picking

And picking

And picking

And picking

And picking

And picking

And picking

And picking

And picking

And

It's something I have to do

I won't let you fall apart

I was there, too (I won't let you fall apart)

Before everything else (I won't let you fall apart)

I was like you (I won't let you fall apart)

Appendix 3 – Page 1 of the Love Letter to Sarka

Dearest Sarka (18SEP2002, Revised 2024):

Well, as you can see, I wrote this a few days ago. I can already see your face upon reading these words, "Oh no, what is Michael up to now?". Or maybe you're becoming a "bit nervous" as you like to say. But fear not Sarka, this is a letter, and yes, it may make you slightly nervous (I hope not) but you don't have to worry. I've got you.

So…why am I writing you a letter? I'm writing you a letter because our 'goodbyes' or our 'goodnights' have always been a bit rushed. Something happens, and the tranquility we've had all day long goes away and we become rushed. Sorry, I'm repeating myself which means I'm a bit nervous. Strange though, don't you think? Because of all of our rapid departures, I wanted to write you this letter so that everything I want and need to say to you, will indeed be said, and not in some rushed, blabbering conversation either.

But first…I need to give you a disclaimer. You are very intelligent, and I do not wish to insult you in any manner. A statement of warning. It sort of prepares the reader or the experiencer for the experience. The first part of this disclaimer involves something you might be doing right now. If you are reading this letter right now and I'm not there with you, then stop! This is meant for me to read it to you and then you can read it for yourself later. Of course, you don't have to listen to me, but I'd really appreciate it if you leave this alone until I have an opportunity to show you how it's intended to be read. With all of it's innuendo, rhythm, inflection, tone, and cadence. Remember, I want to say all of this to you in person. The second part of the disclaimer is this: This is not a love letter! I'm going to say it again: This is not a love letter. That said, you may want to keep this hidden from your recyclable boyfriend (if you plan to keep this at all!) as it could be construed to be a love letter.

Well then. What exactly will this letter be? You and I have had a lot of conversations in the several times we've gone out and I've learned more about you than you might imagine I have. One of the most profound things you said to me (and something I haven't heard in a long time from anyone) is that you still believe in love. You also continued that statement indicating that you believe in honesty, and if that's what this letter will be about, then I have a plethora of honest remarks for you. I have a lot I want to say, so in the event that I'm not permitted to do so, then it will all be right here in this letter like a fucking encyclopedia. Which, if you wanted, you could keep forever. You know, this could be quite comical to you. Just now thought of that. After our night of dancing, I gave you a bunch of CDs, and you very distinctly asked me three times, "What do you want". I still may not answer that question directly because of deductive logic, but after reading this letter, I think you'll be able to figure out exactly what I want.

www.ingramcontent.com/pod-product-compliance
Lightning Source LLC
Chambersburg PA
CBHW070823110726
47973CB00003B/35